371.103 WOL

Parenting Education and Support

New Opportunities

Edited by

Sheila Wolfendale and Hetty Einzig

David Fulton Publishers

London

David Fulton Publishers Ltd
Ormond House, 26–27 Boswell Street, London WC1N 3JD

First published in Great Britain by David Fulton Publishers 1999

Note: The rights of Sheila Wolfendale and Hetty Einzig to be identified as the editors of this work have been asserted by them in accordance with the Copyright, Designs and Patents Act 1988.

Copyright © David Fulton Publishers 1999

British Library Cataloguing in Publication Data
A catalogue record for this book is available from the British Library

ISBN 1–85346–579–8

All rights reserved. No part of this publication may be reproduced, stored in a retrieval system or transmitted, in any form, or by any means, electronic, mechanical, photocopying, recording or otherwise, without the prior permission of the publishers.

Typeset by FSH Print & Production Ltd, London
Printed in Great Britain by the Cromwell Press Ltd, Trowbridge, Wilts.

Contents

Preface   v

Biographical details of contributors   vi

Section One: Review and overview of developments   1

1   Parenting education and the Social Policy Agenda   3
    Gillian Pugh

2   Review of the field: current trends, concepts and issues   13
    Hetty Einzig

3   Families and society: change and continuity   33
    Janet Walker

4   Parents as key determinants in planning and delivering   48
    parenting education and support programmes: an inclusive
    ideology
    Sheila Wolfendale

**Section Two: Themes of parental identity and   59
contexts for parenting**

5   Being a parent: influences and effects upon parenting   61
    from the media
    Lucy McCarraher

6   Going critical: childhood, parenthood and the labour market 75
    Peter Moss

7   The emotional education of parents: attachment theory   90
    and emotional literacy
    James Park

Section Three: Relating principles to practice   105

8   Supporting parents through parenting programmes   107
    Bopinder Samra

9   Support for parents at significant times of transition   122
    Sonya Hinton

10 Parenting education and support: issues in multi-agency   137
    collaboration
    Peter Jones

11 'She wants you to think for yourself, she doesn't want to   150
    give you the answers all the time': parents on parenting
    education and support
    Roger Grimshaw

Index   166

Home and School - A working alliance

This series, edited by *John Bastiani* and *Sheila Wolfendale*, brings together wide-ranging contributions which

- are written from both professional and parental viewpoints
- offer an assessment of what has been achieved
- explore a number of problematic issues and experiences
- illustrate developments that are beginning to take shape.

It appeals to those with a special interest in and commitment to home-school work in all its actual and potential facets.

Series titles

Working with Parents as Partners in SEN
Eileen Gascoigne
1–8534–375–2

Home-School Work in Britain – review, reflection and development
By members of the National Home-School Development Group, edited by John Bastiani and Sheila Wolfendale
1–8534–395–7

Home-School Work in Multicultural Settings
Edited by John Bastiani
1–8534–428–7

Working with Parents of SEN Children after the Code of Practice
Edited by Sheila Wolfendale
1–8534–429–5

Linking Home and School: Partnership in Practice in Primary Education
Hugh and Jenny Waller
1–8534–682–1

The Contribution of Parents to School Effectiveness
Edited by Sheila Wolfendale and John Bastiani
1–85346–633–6

Preface

We would like to thank each of the contributors to this book for having accepted our invitation to contribute a chapter. They have kept to the writing deadlines and accepted our editorial nagging with equanimity and good grace.

The topic area of this book is amongst the priority items on this Government's agenda and is a key part of social policy and strategies across government departments to enhance the quality of life for children and families.

As editors we have aspired to put together a book which describes and reflects upon contemporary thinking and practice in the area of parenting education and support and which, too, identifies emerging ideas and directions in which practice could evolve.

The book is divided into three sections to denote particular emphasis upon themes explored within each of these. Section One: *Review and Overview of Developments* comprises four chapters which together provide a review and critical exploration of the evolution of parenting education and support programmes within the broader, encompassing contexts of family, social and economic policy.

Section Two: *Themes of Parental Identity and Contexts for Parenting* contains three chapters which explore aspects of parental identity, parental tasks and responsibilities, and their place within service provision and decision-making.

The final section, Section Three: *Relating Principles to Practice* contains four chapters which epitomise the relationship between the principles of PES and their translation into practice. Different facets of practice are described, including two grounded within local educational provision, one approach which pursues multi-agency collaboration in the design and delivery of PES, and a final chapter reporting upon the parental perspective on PES.

The chapter authors collectively bring a huge amount of experience and expertise to the area of PES and have backgrounds as educationalists, academics, researchers, practitioners and social policy framers.

We hope that this book can contribute to the formation of a just and effective family policy.

Sheila Wolfendale and Hetty Einzig
London, April 1999

Biographical details of contributors

Hetty Einzig is Research and Development Director of the Parenting Education and Support Forum, having previously been its founding Development Officer. She works nationally in the field of parenting education and support. Prior to this she worked as Research Director of the Artemis Trust developing projects and organisations in the field of psychotherapy and counselling. In this capacity she helped found and develop the Counselling in Primary Care Trust, the National Association of Staff Support and the Information Service of the British Association for Counselling. She has worked as a journalist and writer and is the author of several books, articles, and chapters. She is a trustee of NASS and the Metatonoia Institute and continues to practise as a psychotherapist. She has two children.

Roger Grimshaw is currently Director of Research at the Centre for Crime and Justice Studies, King's College, London. He was formerly a senior researcher at the National Children's Bureau, where he worked on a number of studies of parenting and childcare. He is the author of several books on criminological and child welfare topics; these are fields which he sees as related closely together.

Sonya Hinton is an experienced educational psychologist working for the Surrey Educational Psychology Sevice. She has contributed to undergraduate and postgraduate courses for teachers and psychologists as well as being involved in training special needs assistants, health visitors and pre-school personnel. She has a particular interest in supporting parents through workshops, courses and publications and has also contributed to television and radio programmes for parents including Carlton Television's *Teenagers – a Survival Guide for Parents* and ITV's programmes for parents of pre-schoolers *Everybody's Got One.*

Peter Jones is a community-oriented educational psychologist working in the Plymouth Psychology Service. For five years he coordinated the development of a community-based, multi-agency parenting education and support project in an inner city area of Plymouth. He is a member of the Parenting Forum's executive committee, and jointly chairs its multi-agency working group. His current focus is the role of local multi-agency fora for parenting education and support.

Lucy McCarraher has worked in the print media as a writer, editor and publisher. She has been a television presenter, scriptwriter, script-editor and producer in Australia and the UK. She currently researches and writes on parenting, family issues and work-life balance. She has recently conducted writing and research projects for Exploring Parenthood, Parenting Education and Support Forum, NSPCC, Work-Life Research Centre, National Work-Life Forum, WFD, Sargent Cancer Care for Children, Royal Borough of Kingston's Childcare Audit and has been a Balanced Work Advisor on the Borough's European 'Striking the Balance' project since 1996. She is married with two teenage children.

Peter Moss is Professor of Early Childhood Provision at the Thomas Coram Research Unit, Institute of Education University of London. His research interests include services for children, in particular early childhood services, and the relationship between employment and parenthood; he is co-founder of the Work-Life Research Centre. He has undertaken a wide range of cross-national work, and was Coordinator of the European Commission Childcare Network between 1986 and 1996. His latest book (written with Gunilla Dahlberg and Alan Pence) is *Beyond Quality in Early Childhood Education and Care: Postmodern Perspectives on the Problem with Quality.*

James Park is Director and co-founder of Antidote: Campaign for Emotional Literacy, an organisation which works to promote a more emotionally literate society, in particular by creating an education system that recognises feelings as an integral part of teaching and learning. He is also the author of *Sons, Mothers and Other Lovers* (Little Brown), *Shrinks: The Analysts Analyzed* (Bloomsbury) and *Cultural Icons: Key Figures of the Late Twentieth Century* (Bloomsbury).

Gillian Pugh is Chief Executive of the Thomas Coram Foundation for Children, having previously been Director of the Early Childhood Unit at the National Children's Bureau. She has worked nationally and internationally in the fields of early childhood education and parenting education and support and is author of a number of books including *Confident Parents, Confident Children* and *Learning to be a Parent.* She is a founder member and vice chair of the Parenting Education and Support Forum and a trustee of the National Family and Parenting Institute. She has four children and stepchildren.

Bopinder Samra is Parental Involvement Co-ordinator for the London Borough of Newham's Single Regeneration Budget Raising Achievement Project. Previously she managed and coordinated other projects such as GEST 19: Raising Standards in Inner City Schools and the City Challenge: Action for Achievement Extension Project through which she organised and ran a number of parenting skills programmes. She has also been a secondary school teacher and a Home–School Liaison teacher where she undertook the responsibility of involving ethnic minority parents in schools and in their own learning. She has immense experience of working with parents from a wide variety of backgrounds. She is a trustee of the Parenting Education and Support Forum.

Janet Walker is Professor of Family Policy and Director of the Centre for Family Studies at the University of Newcastle-upon-Tyne. She has led a wide-ranging research programme since 1985, including studies of divorce, post-divorce parenting, mediation, counselling, family communication, domestic violence, and innovations in juvenile justice. She is currently as Research Director in respect of the information meeting pilots in preparation for the implementation of the Family Law Act 1996.

Sheila Wolfendale has been a primary school teacher and remedial reading teacher, an educational psychologist in several LEAs and is currently Director of a Doctorate in Educational Psychology training programme at the University of East London. She has authored and edited many books, booklets, chapters, articles and handbooks on aspects of special needs, early years, and parental involvement. She was awarded a Professorship in 1988 and in 1995 gained a Ph.D. by published works. She has undertaken national and international consultancy in these areas.

SECTION ONE:

Review and overview of developments

Chapter 1

Parenting education and the Social Policy Agenda

Gillian Pugh

Exactly twenty years ago I was asked to prepare a background paper, including a survey of ongoing activity, for the first national seminar on what was then called 'preparation for parenthood'. The report of that survey and the conference at which it was discussed (Pugh 1980), coinciding as it did with my personal struggles as a first-time parent, started for me a lifelong interest in the support that society owes to parents if children's needs are to be met. The response that greeted the more detailed national study that followed (Pugh and De'Ath 1984) was predictable but none the less irritating. 'Surely parenting is caught, not taught? Parents have been bringing up children since time immemorial – why should they need help now?' It was perfectly reasonable to ask for advice on car maintenance or gardening, but why should anyone need to discuss bringing up children?

In the fifteen years that have passed since then, and particularly in the last two, there has been a considerable change in the climate surrounding parenting and family life and a huge raft of government initiatives designed to impact on children and their parents. To what extent does the current policy climate respond to the issues first identified in the 1970s, how have those issues changed, and what are the challenges as we move into the twenty-first century?

The Needs of Parents and the substantially revised follow-up study *Confident Parents, Confident Children* (Pugh, De'Ath and Smith 1994) started from the premise that bringing up children is the most important and most challenging task that most of us embark on and that, if children are to be given the start in life that they require, society must provide parents with sufficient support to enable them to fulfil their obligations with knowledge, understanding and enjoyment. We defined parenting education as

A range of educational and supportive activities which help parents and prospective parents to understand their own social, emotional, psychological and physical needs and those of their children, and which enhance the relationship between them. These activities help create a supportive environment of services within local communities and help families take advantage of them. (Pugh *et al.* 1994, p.66)

This focus recognised that a society that promotes children's optimal development requires strong families supported by strong communities. Parenting education and support is not only about helping parents adopt positive parenting strategies, but also about supporting parents to become involved in community activities, including their children's schools. The change in title between the two studies reflected a growing recognition of the importance of empowerment, self-esteem and self-confidence in achieving these objectives.

The underpinning principles for parenting education were – and still are – also important. This range of activities was to be available to all parents and prospective parents, with a different emphasis at each stage of the life cycle – for example schools should have a role in preparing young people for family life as part of broader lifeskills programmes; antenatal services should recognise the emotional as well as the physical changes in becoming a parent; parents of teenagers will want different kinds of support than parents of new babies and so on. Importantly, they were to be based on principles which valued and respected different approaches to bringing up children, which empowered parents rather than pointing to deficits, and which were as relevant and appropriate to fathers and boys as they were to mothers and girls. We argued that parenting education and support could offer families a range of knowledge, skills and opportunities for developing self-confidence and discussing attitudes and approaches towards parenting.

The book concluded with a comprehensive 'Agenda for Action' aimed at central government, local authorities, health authorities, schools, voluntary organisations and training agencies.

We were however conscious of two challenges. The first related to the value base of parent education. We noted that

a return to the 'back to basics' doctrines of the moral right has given a new immediacy to the conflict between the family's right to privacy and self-determination as against the State's needs for healthy and productive citizens. Is parent education a means of self control, whereby gender stereotypes are reinfoced, the family is two married parents with two children, adolescents are urged to conform to socially accepted norms of behaviour, and middle class approaches to child-rearing are promulgated? Or can it be a means to social change and personal growth, whereby individuals are given increased encouragement and self-confidence to take greater control over their lives, to break out of traditional roles and to question the status quo? (Pugh *et al.* 1994, p.220)

As parenting and family support move higher up the political agenda, this challenge will intensify.

The second challenge was the danger of taking parenting out of context, and of the need to recognise the critical importance of the 'permitting circumstances' that impact on family life – financial security, employment, adequate housing and good day care, health and education facilities. Whilst many of the policy initiatives outlined in this chapter have been or are likely to be beneficial to children and to families, it is a major indictment of our social welfare system that over the last 20 years we have moved from a situation where one in ten children lived in households below the poverty line, to a current figure of more than one in three. This dramatic increase is partly due to the rise in unemployment and partly to the growth in lone parent households. While the research evidence points to relationships within families as being more important to children's optimum development than family structure (Schaffer 1990), it is nevertheless the case that families headed by lone mothers have suffered disproportionately from reduced income levels.

A changing climate

Fortuitously, 1994 was also the International Year of the Family. In the face of growing media hysteria and moral panic about the 'death of the family', the IYF supported a number of high-profile events around the country, the establishment of a cross-party Parliamentary Group on Parenting, and the publication of wide-ranging consultations on parenting and family life (House of Commons 1994), all of which served to sharpen the focus on the need to support parents rather than castigate them as failures or sinners. The Year also helped to create a climate that was perhaps more ready to listen to the recommendations of the 'Agenda for Action'.

One of the key recommendations was for the establishment of a Forum to act as a focus for information on parenting support and education, for debate, to support those working in the field, to network and to influence policy by building on good practice. Some 18 national organisations working with children and parents came together to set up the Parenting Education and Support Forum, which was launched in 1995 with four key aims:

- to raise awareness of parenting and its critical impact on all aspects of children's development;
- to help change the climate to one where support for parents is seen as normal;
- to create a professional network for those working with children, parents and families in order to share information and expertise;
- to press for coherent policies.

The Forum's success in its first three years, even with very limited resources, is reflected in the government's decision to set up a

National Family and Parenting Institute during 1999 with almost identical aims, and a considerably increased income.

In the five years since 1994, and particularly since the Labour government came to power in 1997, there has been a remarkable shift in the policy agenda as it relates to children and families. What had for so long been the preserve of a small minority of researchers, practitioners and campaigners, mainly within the voluntary sector, has rapidly become a focus of interest for politicians, practitioners and the media. Increasingly the family has been identified as the key site not only for support, but also for intervention and, as the chapters in this book illustrate, across a wide range of professional interests. There is space here to pick out only a few of the key initiatives, which can variously be described as intervention, prevention, support, promotion or empowerment. The complexity of these different discourses is discussed by Peter Jones in Chapter 10.

An overarching theme of much of the recent policy development has been that of prevention, and particularly primary prevention – the notion that simple, relatively inexpensive measures, put into effect early, can save the need for more complex interventions later (Sinclair et al. 1997). Drawing on research on the relationship between particular parenting styles and poor outcomes for children, parenting education has been seen as a means of preventing later difficulties in a whole range of areas from family breakdown (Utting 1995) to juvenile offending (Utting et al. 1993), and from mental ill health (Mental Health Foundation, 1999) to child abuse (National Commission 1996). A preventive approach has also underpinned the 'refocusing' initiative from the Department of Health, in which the Department has used its own research (Department of Health 1995) and that of the Audit Commission (1994) to encourage social service departments to shift some resources away from the very costly work on child protection towards a broader approach to family support.

A further theme of these studies on prevention has been the importance of working across agencies to provide a holistic service for children and families. The main policy outcome from this drive towards more coherent planning for children has been the introduction of Children's Services Plans (Hearn and Sinclair 1998), requiring social services to work with health and education in planning services for all children, but particularly for those with the greatest level of need. A complementary development has been the requirement to establish Early Years Development and Child Care partnerships in all local authorities (DfEE 1998a).

The agenda for education and health has tended to focus on promotion or empowerment rather than prevention or intervention. In parallel with the growing recognition of parents' role in their children's development has been an acceptance of the growing body of research on the critical importance of the first five years of children's lives for all aspects of later development. This research has been supplemented most recently by evidence on early brain development which points to the impact that the environment has on the developing brain in the first few months of life (Carnegie Corporation 1994, Shore 1997). The widely quoted research from HighScope in the United States (Schweinhart and Weikart 1993), in which over a 25 year period some $7 was saved in welfare expenditure for every $1 invested in early education, has two equally compelling messages. Not only are high quality early education programmes important, but so too is the involvement and support of parents in their children's education. The expansion of nursery education, the 'Early Excellence Centre' programme, the Sure Start initiative and the Family Learning Initiative all reflect the research evidence on early learning and on parents' role as their children's first and most important educator.

One other important area of research which is having a renewed impact on both policy and practice is attachment theory (see James Park in Chapter 7, and Howe 1999). Bowlby's (1982) work on the central importance of a child's early attachment to a parent or carer if he or she is to develop a secure sense of self and emotional equilibrium has tended to be dismissed by those who have interpreted it as requiring mothers to stay at home full time to care for their pre-school children. This was never Bowlby's intention, however, and attachment theory does make an important contribution to our growing understanding of the importance of social and emotional competence as the basis of self-esteem, and of the role of the emotions in children's and adults' learning. Whilst early-years educators have always understood that this is the foundation stone for all learning, it has been less evident at later stages of the curriculum. The curriculum review of personal, health and social education undertaken by the Department for Education and Employment and the Department of Health for the Qualifications and Curriculum Authority as part of the wider review of the National Curriculum is to be welcomed. It is also central to the Department for Education's Green Paper on lifelong learning *The Learning Age* (DfEE 1998b).

There is thus evidence that at least some of the unprecedented number of recent government initiatives have used research as the basis for new policy developments, and that children and families are amongst those to benefit most from the government's attempts to create joined up solutions to joined up problems.

Supporting families

But to what extent are the new initiatives based on the underpinning principles outlined above. The government's Green Paper *Supporting Families*, published by the Ministerial Group on the

Family chaired by the Home Secretary and drawing in all the key government departments, recognised the danger of government interference in family life, but also the responsibilities of government (Home Office 1998). The principles underlying the Green Paper's proposals for family policy are consistent with our own: that the interests of children are paramount; that children need stability and security; and that government should support parents in supporting their children. Five areas are covered:

1. Ensuring all families have access to advice and support

The proposals here are wide-ranging and include the National Family and Parenting Institute and the £540m Sure Start scheme noted above, as well as a new national parenting helpline, an enhanced role for health visitors, additional suport for parents to learn with their children through family literacy and mentoring schemes, introduction of education for parenthood in the school curriculum, support for grandparents, and improved adoption legislation.

Much of this builds on current good practice and is to be warmly welcomed. The ambitious Sure Start scheme is described by government as demonstrating a commitment to 'tackling complex issues in radical, innovative ways. All the evidence shows that early intervention and support can help to reduce family breakdown, strengthen children's readiness for school; and benefit society in the longer term by preventing social exclusion, regenerating communities and reducing crime. Inside the home, we want to offer support to enable parents to strengthen the bond with their children; outside it, we want to help families make the most of the local services on offer.'

Sure Start, which will provide services for parents and children under three in 250 high need areas, is grounded in evidence from child development and attachment theory, as well as evidence of what works in supporting families with young children within communities – the importance of non-stigmatising mainstream services, outreach work, informal support for parents and so on.

The National Family and Parenting Institute faces a stiffer challenge, for although it is to be independent of government, it will inevitably be seen by some as the voice of the nanny state telling parents how to bring up children. Much will depend on the extent to which it can build on and work with the Parenting Forum, which has grown from ongoing work in the field.

2. Better financial support for families

The ambitious aim here is to reduce child poverty through initiatives such as increased child benefits, Working Families Tax Credit, the New Deal for Lone Parents and the reform of the Child Support

Agency. More recently, the 1999 Budget announced that by 2001 the married couple's allowance will be replaced by a children's tax credit, a move that has been argued for over many years by those working in the children's field. It is too soon to assess the success of these initiatives, but given the number of children living on or below the poverty line, this continuing redistribution of resources must be welcomed.

3. Helping families balance work and home

The main initiatives here are the increase in childcare places through the National Childcare Strategy, family friendly employee rights (including fairer working hours, flexible working arrangements, parental leave and time off for family reasons) and promoting family-friendly employment practice.

There are those who argue that this government has put too strong an emphasis on work and a requirement to work (Jack and Jordan, in press), but the moves to bring the UK into line with Europe in enabling parents to achieve a better balance between employment and bringing up their children are long overdue. If the proposals for parental leave are to be taken up by low income families, it will need to be paid leave, as it is in many other European countries.

4. Strengthening marriage

The proposals for strengthening marriage are more controversial, as the Green Paper recognises in stating that families do not want to be lectured about their relationships. The emphasis on supporting relationships and on reducing conflict in relationship breakdown, especially when children are involved, is however welcome. The emphasis in the 1996 Family Law Act on mediation, on handling disputes over children and on children remaining in contact with both parents is important, although a new integrated court welfare service will be required if the recommendations are to be implemented.

5. Better support for serious family problems

The proposals here cover truancy and exclusions, work with children with behavioural problems, youth offending, teenage pregnancy and domestic violence. Limitations of space prevent a detailed analysis of these wide-ranging issues, but two points must be made. The first relates to the requirements under the 1998 Crime and Disorder Act for parenting orders to be imposed on parents where their child or young person has been convicted of an offence. The Green Paper claims that 'the parenting order will help parents change offending behaviour by their children'. One must question the value of these orders, given the lack of evidence either that compulsory parenting education is effective, or that parents can so easily change the behaviour of their adolescent children. There is also concern that the child curfew proposals contravene the UN Convention on the Rights of the Child.

The second concerns domestic violence, where government support for the proposed action to reduce the levels of such violence are sadly not coupled with an equal commitment to reduce levels of violence against children through legislation to ban physical punishment in the home (see the Children are Unbeatable campaign referred to in the end of chapter References).

In conclusion

The Green Paper represents a serious attempt by government to shift the public policy agenda towards children and families. Together with the Quality Protects initiative, which requires local authorities to take a more responsible approach to their role as corporate parents for the children in their care, it is an encouraging response to the 'Agenda for Action' published in 1994. A number of challenges however remain:

- Recognising that children's rights and parents' wishes will not always coincide.
- The very high expectations raised by the current agenda.
- The importance of a continuing commitment to income distribution, particularly reforming the tax and benefit system to support families with dependent children.
- The need to develop a culture based on empowerment and choice, not on deficiencies and social control.
- Broadening the current agenda to take account of a number of key players whose voices are seldom heard – particularly listening to the views of children, and finding more successful ways of involving fathers, and parents from minority ethnic groups.
- Ensuring that policy is, wherever possible, based on evidence of what works (see for example Lloyd 1999).
- Realising that the most powerful interventions are those that combine support for parents with high quality early education for children.
- Building on the role of schools, both in developing personal, social and health education curricula for all pupils, and in forging closer relationships with parents.
- Ensuring that access to services remains a high priority.
- Developing a framework for training and accreditation of parenting education workers.

- Making sure that the thinking – and the planning and service provision – really is joined up.

A review of research on prevention and early intervention undertaken for the cross-departmental spending review which led to the establishment of Sure Start (Pugh 1998): concluded that there were four groups of protective factors which helped children in adverse circumstances achieve good outcomes:

- An adequate standard of living.
- Temperament or disposition that attract and encourage caregiving, lead to high self-esteem, sociability and autonomy, ability to solve problems, and an internal locus of control.
- Dependable caregivers: growing up in a family with one or two dependable adults whose childrearing practices are positive and appropriate; a warm family and the absence of family discord.
- Networks of community support: living in a supportive and safe community; a peer group which is prosocial; and schools where children are valued and learning is encouraged.

As the review concluded, we know enough about what works to make a difference to children's lives. Let us not miss this opportunity to do so.

References

Audit Commission (1994) *Seen But Not Heard: Coordinating community child health and social services for children in need.* London: Audit Commission.

Bowlby, J. (1982) *Attachment.* London: Hogarth Press.

Carnegie Corporation (1994) *Starting Points: Meeting the needs of our youngest children.* New York: Carnegie Corporation.

Children are Unbeatable. An alliance of organisations seeking legal reform to give children the same protection under the law on assault as adults and promoting positive, non-violent discipline. 77 Holloway Road, London N7 8JZ.

DfEE (1998a) *Early Years Development and Childcare Partnership Planning Guidance 1999–2000.* London: DfEE.

DfEE (1998b) *The Learning Age: A renaissance for a new Britain.* London: Stationery Office.

Department of Health (1995) *Child Protection: Messages from Research.* London: HMSO.

Einzig, H. (1998) 'The promotion of successful parenting: an agenda for action', in Utting, D. (ed.) *Children's Services Now and in the Future.* London: National Children's Bureau.

Hearn, B. and Sinclair, R. (1998) *Children's Services Plans, Analysing Need: Re-Allocating Resources. A Report to the Department of Health.* London: National Children's Bureau.

Home Office (1998) *Supporting Families, A Consultation Paper.* London: Stationery Office.

House of Commons (1994) All Party Parliamentary Group on Parenting and International Year of the Family UK, *Parliamentary Hearings*.

Howe, D. (1999) *Attachment Theory, Child Maltreatment and Family Support: A practice and assessment model*. London: Macmillan Press.

Jack, G. and Jordan, B. (in press) 'Social capital and the protection of children', *Children & Society* **13**.

Lloyd, E. (ed.) (1999) *What Works in Parenting Education*. Barkingside: Barnardo's.

Mental Health Foundation (1999) *Bright Futures: promoting children and young people's mental health*. London: Mental Health Foundation.

National Commission of Inquiry into the Prevention of Child Abuse (1996) *Childhood Matters*, volumes 1 and 2, chair Williams, G. London: Stationery Office.

Pugh, G. (ed.) (1980) *Preparation for Parenthood*. London: National Children's Bureau.

Pugh, G. (1998) 'Children at risk of becoming socially excluded'. Treasury Seminar, 21 January 1998.

Pugh, G. and De'Ath, E. (1984) *The Needs of Parents: policy and practice in parent education*. London: Macmillan.

Pugh, G., De'Ath, E., Smith, C. (1994) *Confident Parents, Confident Children: policy and practice in parenting education and support*. London: National Children's Bureau.

Schaffer, R (1990) *Making Decisions About Children*. Oxford: Blackwell.

Schweinhart, L. and Weikart, D. (1993) *A Summary of Significant Benefits: The High/Scope Perry Pre-school through age 27*. Ypsilanti: High/Scope.

Shore R (1997) *Rethinking the Brain: new insights into early development*. New York: Families and Work Institute.

Sinclair, R., Hearn, B. and Pugh, G. (1997) *Preventive Work with Families: the role of mainstream services*. London: National Children's Bureau.

Smith, C. and Pugh, G. (1996) *Learning to be a Parent*. London: Family Policy Studies Centre.

Utting D (1995) *Family and Parenthood: supporting families and preventing breakdown*. York: Joseph Rowntree Foundation.

Utting, D., Bright, J. and Henricson, C. (1993) *Crime and the Family: improving childrearing and preventing delinquency*. London: Family Policy Studies Centre.

Chapter: 2

Review of the field: current trends, concepts and issues

Hetty Einzig

Summary

I have written elsewhere about the complexity and multi-level nature of parenting (Einzig 1996) and the need therefore for policy approaches to be equally multi-dimensional and sensitive (Einzig 1998a). This chapter looks more closely at current trends in practice and patterns of provision in parenting education and support; at underpinning theories and issues of evaluation and the current debate around 'what works' in prevention fuelled by the political demand for immediate solutions to what are complex social problems. It concludes with a plea for an Integrative Model of provision with a promotional focus.

Introduction: revisiting definitions and principles

What exactly constitutes parenting education and support? The development, promotion and awareness of parenting education and support has been patchy, with no consistent approach, national strategy or long-term financial underpinning (Pugh *et al.* 1994). To some extent this is still the national picture. But also much has changed. Given the intense policy focus on families and on supporting parents as an intervention to ameliorate a range of social problems (see Chapter 1), it is a good moment to re-examine some of the issues raised by the current debate on parenting education and how we might find our way around this complex, broad based and rapidly developing field.

Parenting education and support is a generic term for a hugely diverse range of learning opportunities for parents. The best established definition was provided in *Confident Parents, Confident Children* (Pugh *et al.* 1994, see Chapter 1, p. 3) It takes a broad view and conceives of education and support as indivisible, where education is non-didactic but means 'learning in its fullest sense of growing in knowledge, skills, understanding and personal development' (Parenting Education and Forum 1997a). This view of parenting education and support also maintains that there is no single most effective approach or 'best buy', just as there is no blue print for the 'happy' family (Smith 1996). Approaches therefore must be based on rigorous principles to ensure ethical practice and an empowerment model of intervention, not a deficit or coercive one (Smith and Pugh 1996). Principles include the concept of parental responsibility and respect for family and cultural diversity. Parenting is seen as a continuous process and an interactive one, between parent and child and others, and is concerned with the development of the whole person.

In this period of increasing focus on the family and parenting as areas of intervention it is important to remind ourselves of these principles of parenting education and support and their breadth. Concern about children's mental health (Mental Health Foundation 1999) and educational attainment (DfEE 1997), about the development of boys and the rise in disaffection in young men (Downes 1997, Phillips 1993, Home Office 1998a), about the rising divorce rate and its implications for the health of all family members (see Chapter 3), about the increasingly stressful juggling of both men and women in trying to balance work and home life – and a range of other issues relating to the family – may lead us to seek quick solutions. Our better understanding of the fundamental importance of the parent–child relationship has led policy makers to look expectantly to the field of parenting education, in particular group based short-term programmes, for some answers to these urgent social problems.

Current UK trends

Current trends in parenting education and support fall into two strands: those that are evolving on the ground, in the community or are locally led: 'bottom up'; and those that come from the 'top down', led or influenced by policy makers and medical and academic professionals. The two strands come together in the huge growth in group-based parenting programmes.

Group-based parenting programmes

The widespread growth in group-based parenting programmes, run mostly by the voluntary or private sectors, was fuelled in 1996 by the publication of the study by Smith, *Developing Parenting Programmes* (Smith 1996), thereafter attracting increasing interest from researchers and policy makers in their effectiveness as an intervention. The cost benefits of group work are clear and attractive but also the 'added value' derived from the support network of participants created within groups have made group interventions increasingly popular. Most recent research indicates that group work can be more effective in terms of measurable outcomes than one-to-one work (Barlow 1997, Webster-Stratton 1997, 1999), but the debate as to which kind of groups 'work' continues.

Growth of innovative and multi-agency projects

There has been considerable growth of a range of family and parent support projects over the last four years within all sectors, voluntary, statutory and private (see also Chapter 10). While many of these are still one-off projects, driven by a determined and charismatic individual working in isolation (Kordan 1999), a growing number are grounded in strategic local authority, multi-agency or community partnerships. National schemes such as the Pre-School Learning Alliance Life Long Learning Millennium fund and now Sure Start and the Home Office family support grants will increase the number and viability of small-scale innovative projects set up by and serving local communities. Those set up under these national schemes will hopefully be well evaluated, so providing lessons for future projects.

The trend towards multi-agency projects, many of them community driven, gives cause for optimism that support for parents and parenting may become more embedded in social structures and local policies. One example is the Shankill Road Early Years Project (Greater Shankill Partnership Company Limited 1996) which is based within a multiply deprived area of North Belfast. In an area of over 50 per cent unemployment and a devastated infrastructure for housing and work this community regeneration project (which brings together education, health and social services) has started where people's hearts and anxieties are most engaged: their children. With a range of support and learning opportunities, including childcare, preschools, parenting education groups and play groups, parents' self-esteem, confidence and levels of engagement have been raised, enabling them to participate in developing further training and job opportunities, seeking and buying in the specialist professional help they need at each stage. For a more in-depth look at multi-agency early years projects see Virginia Makin's study (1997).

Other examples include the Family Links project in Oxfordshire (Family Links 1997) which works with teachers, parents and children within schools; many of the Barnardo's projects both here and in Northern Ireland (Lloyd *et al.* 1997); the parenting forum and other projects in Rotherham where parents, having been brought in at very early stages of policy and practice development, are now informed, articulate and discriminating in their demands, thus able to participate fully in planning services (Pinder 1999).

Growth in local groups and fora

The number of local groups and fora bringing together a range of providers of child, family and parenting services at local and regional level has grown rapidly over the last five years. The Parenting Forum listed local fora in almost every area of England by 1999. Scotland established a parenting forum, with constitutional links to the Parenting Education & Support Forum, in 1997, Northern Ireland launched one in 1999 and Wales launched a network for parenting in February 1999.

Fathers

There is a growing interest in the role of fathers in family life and specifically in the upbringing of boys. Concern about the long hours men work in Britain and the detriment of this to family life has been heightened by concerns over the rise in boys' disaffection from school and learning, the rise of juvenile crime and the role that fathers might play in helping to alter this trend (Burgess 1997, Home Office 1998a). Initiatives addressing fathers' needs directly are poised to burgeon as the Home Office Family Support Grants have identified men, boys and fathers as their special theme for funding for 1999.

'Drivers': patterns of local provision

Parenting education is currently delivered and funded by a number of different organisations including:

- Local education authorities, via educational psychology services, schools and preschool services, parent partnership programmes.
- Health authorities, health trusts and community health trusts, child guidance units.
- Social services departments (mainly nurseries and family centres)
- Voluntary organisations.
- Churches and other faith groups.
- Home Office (via Young Offender Institutions and prisons).
- Academic institutions.
- Private businesses (usually for marketing and dissemination).
(Smith 1996)

And increasingly, independent individuals have set up their own programmes or support groups (e.g. Murphy 1996, Pitt 1998).

Involvement for each agency may be based on different considerations, such as policy demands, budget cuts, changes and shifting priorities in service delivery and funding for short-term projects which may have particular eligibility criteria or targets. The problem for developing parenting education and support is the general lack of cohesive planning at policy level and the subsequent lack of coordinated service delivery.

When one looks at a local area in detail it is clear that for historical and funding reasons different 'drivers' emerge in different localities, shaping the trends outlined above and thus leading to very different patterns of local provision for parents and families. The development of projects and initiatives may be driven by an individual's vision, professional training or theoretical orientation; development may be driven by community need, by policy or legislation or by funding source and pattern of funding. Each of these elements, once established as the main driving force, will have a different but profound impact on the kind of provision and pattern of support that develops in a particular area over the long term: on whether parents are involved as partners in the development, whether a project is sustainable, and what kind of outputs are expected (Einzig and Kordan 1999).

A recent study undertaken by the Parenting Forum (Kordan 1999) for the Mental Health Foundation as part of their National Inquiry into the mental health of children and young people (Mental Health Foundation 1999) looked in detail at three local areas: Oxfordshire, Southern Derbyshire and the London Borough of Newham. It paints a complex picture of development and provision. Analysis reveals strong regional patterns whose characteristic 'flavour' may impact on service provision and local understanding of parenting support in these three areas for years to come (Einzig 1998b).

The 'drivers' in Oxfordshire come from education, in particular early years and community education, with strong voluntary sector involvement. A range of local fora and projects are coordinated by a multi-agency Early Years Forum. Projects are encouraged to be outcome oriented in their thinking. In Southern Derbyshire by contrast, parenting education and support was initiated and continues to be driven by health promotion, with a focus on positive parenting as part of good mental health. Voluntary organisations have a lower profile here. In general, the focus in Southern Derbyshire is to change perceptions. Explicitly, the aim is to facilitate parents and practitioners in creating a philosophy of parenting and a vision for health. This is embedded in local policy (e.g. the promotion of non-violence). There is a strong psychodynamic orientation in approaches and an emphasis on building foundations and on information and resources rather than outputs.

Newham, an inner London borough with a large ethnic mix, has a number of deprived areas qualifying for Single Regeneration Bid and City Challenge funding (see Chapter 8). Funding, in this instance City Challenge funding, has been the recent driver in shaping local provision. Support and education for parents has been one of the borough's top priorities. The focus here is predominantly on support for parents (see p. 20) with support for parenting developed as an additional resource (see Chapter 8), on parental involvement in children's education and on parents as learners with short-term adult education programmes for parents offering progression routes into vocational education.

Concepts and theories

Theoretical underpinnings

In keeping with the diversity of provision and range of professionals involved in delivery parenting education has developed from a number of theoretical bases. This impacts on evaluation since one is rarely comparing like with like, or the same desirable outcomes. The main underpinning theories to parenting education interventions are the following:

- **Behavioural:** emphasises skills learning, often with behaviour modification or management of the child as stimulus and goal; often the approach used with children with conduct disorders and their families (Webster-Stratton and Taylor 1998).
- **Cognitive:** emphasises the role and ability of the mind to re-conceptualise our beliefs and approaches to problems if given the right information and structure (Janis-Norton 1997, Puckering *et al.* 1994).
- **Adlerian:** based on the work of Josef Adler who developed concepts of power and our need for control. Emphasises respect for the child and its striving for power in the individuation process; this approach puts the child, its needs and an understanding of the need behind the behaviour, at the centre of the work (Smith 1996).
- **Psychodynamic:** based on the work of Freud, Jung, Klein, Winnicott and other psychoanalysts who place a primacy on the role of the past to shape our psyche and current behaviour patterns; also on the role of reflection and understanding of the past in bringing about change (Daws 1989, Howell *et al.* 1997).
- **Humanistic:** emphasises a collaborative, partnership approach, the building of supportive alliances and networks, the sharing of experiences. Tends to be non-goal orientated (Parr 1996, Davis and Hester 1996).
- **Attachment Theory:** emphasises the early attachment relationship between parent and child and the need to create a secure environment in the parenting education context for trust, learning and change to take place and in order to help foster a secure attachment in the repair of the damaged parent–child relationship. (see Chapter 7 for detailed description and references).

Resilience and attachment

As described above there is a rise in multi-agency and community based projects, the roots of which one can trace back to Bronfenbrenner's ecological model (1979). Others have talked of the importance of parenting being seen in the context of the 'permitting circumstances' (Rutter 1974). Environmental, social and economic factors have, as we know, a major impact on outcomes for children and on all parents' capacity to do an adequate job. The increasing numbers of children and their parents living in poverty and the consequences of this on children's health, development and educational achievement have been well documented and demand macro-economic solutions.

However, the concept of resilience has an important part to play in the discourse of parenting support. Resilience is central to an individual's capacity to thrive, whatever the circumstances. Rutter defines resilience as involving several related elements, including

- self-esteem;
- self-confidence;
- a belief in one's own self-efficacy;
- ability to deal with change and adaptation;
- repertoire of social problem-solving approaches.

(Rutter 1987, p.607, cited in Fundudis 1997)

These add up to, in other words, the 'personal psychological resources' of the individual (Belsky 1984, cited in Fundudis 1997).

Studies of families in adverse circumstances show resilience to be linked to two key factors: the quality of the relationship between parents and children and supportive community networks. Thus resilience is not a fixed quality, dependent solely on the cards that have been dealt to one. 'Genetic advantages are useful but as social beings in the modern world our greatest advantage is to be able to know our own minds and those of others, and therefore to stand up for something or someone...' (Kraemer 1998). Resilience is fostered by parents and family, but also by school and community (Belsky and Isabella 1988, cited in Svanberg 1998).

An individual's resilience and outcomes later on are very strongly determined by early experiences with caregivers when patterns of attachment are laid down (Kraemer 1997). These attachments create a mental map in the child of how they will be responded to and cared for when distressed, hungry, afraid and how their anger, joy, love and naughtiness will be received and dealt with. The mental map thus formed guides all future intimate relationships and recent research has demonstrated how these attachments are transmitted across generations (Steele 1997 and Chapter 7 of this volume).

It is important to stress that secure attachments are primarily but not only forged in the early years. While clearly it is harder to put right later what has gone wrong at an early stage, adolescence is a key moment when remedial work can be done – when young people need and seek guidance from parents or other significant adults based on a supportive and trustworthy relationship (Coleman and Roker 1998 and Chapter 9 of this volume). This has increasingly important implications for teachers and for their training and for the need to view young people not as a problem but full of resources.

Although current research shows disadvantages from a single parent family model, it appears that the reasons for this are largely economic and may also be related to current Western work patterns, family norms and social expectations. Ultimately research tells us that no particular family structure will guarantee the development of secure attachments or that the parenting needs of children are met (see Chapter 3). What is important is the nature and quality of the parenting. It is this and other key intimate relationships and supportive community networks that foster secure attachments and resilience (Rutter 1987, cited in Fundudis 1997).

The attachment paradigm as a framework for the development of primary prevention and early intervention has been recognised and proposed in the 1997 Health Select Committee. 'Enabling and facilitating social competence, self-esteem and secure attachments is likely to create the conditions for a post-industrial society where relationships are based on mutual recognition and respect rather than on fear or deference' (Svanberg 1998, p.567).

Support for parents, support for parenting

In understanding this diverse field of activity there is a useful distinction to be made between support for parents and support for parenting (Einzig 1998a).

Support for parents recognises parents both in their parenting role and as individuals with their own developmental and here-and-now needs. Interventions include community support projects like drop-in centres, outreach work like Home Start UK (Shinman 1994), school initiatives such as home–school liaison (Bastiani and Wolfendale 1996), supportive employment practices, further training opportunities, safe play areas for children (Play Council 1998), and economic measures. There is a growth of projects that focus on support for parents almost exclusively and there is evidence that often small-scale, practical interventions and services can have a significant impact on raising parental self-esteem, confidence and agency (Gibbons 1991, Barnes 1999).

The question then arises as to whether raising parental well-being through environmental and practical support measures will have an impact on parenting style, enhance parental relationships with their children and help them be more effective parents. This is an area that has received little attention from researchers largely because such interventions are notoriously hard to measure.

Support for parenting, on the other hand, focuses on the emotional and psychological aspects of bringing up children and recognises that the care of children involves not just parents but others who have a close and influential relationship with the child: carers, early years workers, siblings, grandparents and other relations, teachers. The impetus is educative and the aim is either to enhance the skills and understanding of those who wish to be 'better parents' (Smith 1996) or to alter negative or abusive parenting patterns towards a positive style of parenting, one that will better support the child's developmental needs. Much activity here is group based with some provision of individual work for those in need of intensive support: for example of the NEWPIN centre which combines group and individual work for families on the brink of crisis (Jenkins-Hansen 1997).

In practice support for parents and support for parenting often overlap: an example is the Thomas Coram Foundation project model (Pugh in press, see also Makins 1997) – but perhaps not as often, or as strategically, as they could.

Because emotions run high in the parenting process the relationships between those working with families and the parents they work with can be intimate, intense and charged with expectation on both sides. It is important, particularly with the rapid growth of provision, to increase our understanding of the emotional and psychological processes at work in these interactions if services are to be sensitive, flexible and effective and practitioners are not to be overwhelmed. For example both of the approaches to support described above draw on the powerful process of modelling: the group facilitator, outreach worker or counsellor models in their interactions with the parent, family or children a way of relating that is positive, non-abusive, respectful, and effective (see also Behr 1997 and the use of video-taped scenarios, Webster-Stratton and Taylor 1998). Just as the child emulates the parent so the parent hopefully absorbs this positive way of relating during interactions with the 'worker' and is able to reproduce it at home, thus conveying it in turn to the child and effecting positive changes in parent–child and family relationships. Modelling only happens where there is relationship, where some form of attachment has developed (see Chapter 7); it is not associated with behaviour modification techniques (see below).

Many feedback questionnaires and other evaluations of group programmes attest to the fact that parents come to feel listened to, understood and valued through the group process alone, aside from any discrete skills they may have been overtly taught (Smith 1996, Grimshaw and McGuire 1998 and see Chapter 11 of this volume). Until recently there has been less attention paid to the power of this emotional process and its educative potential within the practical approaches to support for parents, and the development of services.

The attention now being paid to family learning and lifelong learning (Alexander 1998) allied with greater awareness of the emotional foundations to the learning process (Goleman 1996, Gottman 1997) are starting to alert us to the educative potential that lies within the supportive process in itself. An understanding of this process is drawing attention since the wealth of research into attachment theory and the most recent inter-generational attachment research have begun to be more widely disseminated and incorporated into practice.

What works? – parent training versus parenting education

While in practice in Britain some or all of the theoretical models and concepts outlined above may be combined in parenting programmes developed from the 'bottom up', there is a trend from 'top down' professional and policy development, towards a polarisation between what is termed 'parent training' (targeted approaches) and 'parenting education' (broader, open access approach). This is led by the United States, where the field is more established and better funded. American paediatrician, Nicholas Long (1997) describes the 'third generation of parent education'. He sees the first phase as largely dependent on extended family and local community support and the second as marked by the growth in sales of books by childcare gurus, the growth in extra-familial parent education programmes and in research studies that supported their effectiveness. In this third phase Long sees the focus on outcomes becoming paramount, along with issues of cost effectiveness and improved facilitator training coming to the fore.

'Parent training' emerges from the medical model, using behaviour modification techniques, developed by clinicians, to address medically identified oppositional and conduct disorders or antisocial behaviours. It targets specific groups of parents and children deemed to be 'high risk' or failing, usually operating within a clinical setting and sets specific measurable outcomes. Several programmes, using behavioural approaches within clinical settings, have been well funded and thoroughly evaluated, particularly in the USA (Webster-Stratton 1999, Utting *et al.* 1993, Kazdin 1990 cited in Long 1997). Some programmes developed within this model have been applied in educational settings and offer specific attainment targets (Janis-Norton 1997).

In this picture 'parenting education' lies at the other extreme. It has tended to develop within the voluntary sector in response to consumer demand, aimed at those parents who are concerned but without clinically defined problems. Programmes offer a variety of approaches, often drawing on a number of theoretical models as outlined above but based on goals of improving relationships and understanding, shared learning and an emphasis on process rather than outcomes. In between, of course, lie a range of different programmes with more or less specific target outcomes in the educational, social and mental health spheres.

A notable exception to this polarisation is the work of Philip and Carolyn Cowan at the University of Berkeley, California. They have conducted a well-funded long-term research programme for first time parents with matched samples in intervention and control groups. The parenting education happens within groups facilitated by couples following a roughly humanistic/psychodynamic model and has been shown on a number of clinical measures to be effective in improving couple outcomes (Cowan and Cowan 1991). The latest research shows the programme to be having a positive impact on children's ability at 5 years to manage the transition to school with high prediction rates based on base line assessments (Cowan and Cowan 1998, unpublished research in progress).

A polarisation between a 'training' model for parents and an 'educative' one is beginning to make itself felt in Britain following the political demands for speedy solutions to achieve juvenile crime reduction targets and for specific educational targets to raise reading, writing and maths attainment. These problems are complex and urgent but also highly politically embarrassing, hence the demand for answers that are seen to be tough, quick, and effective. Parents, identified as crucial in ameliorating their children's educational and social chances, are thus being targeted. The parent training model is clinically respectable, offering identifiable, time limited, cost-effective interventions with well evaluated short-term outcomes (short term is of course a major attraction in a political framework).

In the light of such legislation as the parenting orders provision of the Crime and Disorder Act (which mandates for parenting 'classes' for parents of offending youngsters) (Home Office 1998b) it is reasonable to fear that political pressure may start to shape provision, particularly if behaviour modification methods continue to be identified by some researchers as the 'active ingredient' in parenting education (cited in Svanberg 1998).

Some of the concerns about behavioural approaches come from psychodynamically trained clinicians who experience them as mechanistic and lacking in sensitivity (Webster-Stratton and Taylor 1998). While behavioural interventions score high in evaluation studies notes of caution have been sounded about taking too narrow an approach to parenting support: in his review of parent management training as a treatment for oppositional and aggressive behaviours Kazdin (1997 cited in Barnes 1999) found it to be effective but he also noted a high drop-out rate of parents. In her systematic review of the effectiveness of parent training programmes in improving the behaviour of 3 to 7 year olds Barlow found that groups using behavioural methods were effective but that at follow-up (between 6 months and 3 years) as many as 50 per cent of mothers still reported problems (Barlow 1997).

In summary, the current debate around 'what works' in parenting education is in danger of being reduced to a polarised argument between advocates of a universal open-access primary prevention approach, often via programmes which emphasise emotional understanding as needing to precede behavioural change ('parenting education'), and those who favour the medical model of targeted programmes utilising behavioural techniques finely honed in the clinic with the single focus goal of managing children's aggressive or dysfunctional behaviour ('parent training').

The first 'camp' is criticised for being too costly and its programmes for being poorly, if at all, evaluated; the second 'camp' raises concerns over its narrow goals (possibly at the expense of understanding and emotional growth), coercive methods and for the danger of creating a stigmatising service by targeting parents deemed to have failed.

This polarisation is simplistic and ultimately does not serve parents, children and families. We need to start asking what works for whom, where, when, how and why before we can even begin to move forward in our understanding (Barnes 1999).

In the UK currently most parenting education contains an integration of cognitive, behavioural, humanistic and psychodynamic approaches in its four key elements:

- information
- skills learning
- sharing experiences
- opportunities to reflect on the past.

(Einzig 1998)

Some programmes now hold these elements within an attachment theory framework, for example the Family Nurturing Network (Dean and Klimes 1998).

This Integrative Model sees behavioural problems not as sharply distinct from 'normal' children's behaviour or family functioning but on a spectrum (Stewart-Brown 1998). An integrative approach is seen as inherently valuable because it raises emotional understanding and 'literacy' (Goleman 1996 and Chapter 7 of this volume).

An integrative approach to parenting education is important not just because parents find it supportive and enhancing but also because it may yield longer-term outcomes in helping parents to be more aware of the parenting process and the parent–child relationship. This understanding may well equip parents to cope better with their children's developmental stages over the long term and may therefore significantly contribute to their children's attainment and mental health in later years. By definition behavioural skills taught to address specific problems that manifest in age-related ways can contribute in only a very limited way to a life cycle approach to supporting parents.

We do not yet have definitive answers to the question of whether parenting education based on an Integrative Model works, and for whom, when and why. Aside from parent satisfaction questionnaires and a few high quality but small and comparatively short-term studies (Parr 1996, Davis and Hester 1996), evaluations of British programmes with a broader based educational aim operating within a humanistic, psychodynamic or attachment framework are as yet insufficient to create a convincing and critical mass.

Cost benefit analysis

This, of course, is the thorniest problem of all. To determine not just what works for whom but whether the intervention is cost effective requires complex research designs conducted over the long term.

The most well-known research study that showed cost benefits is the Perry School/High Scope project which studied a group of children who received the High Scope model of preschool education over a period of almost 30 years, showing that for every $1 spent more than $7 were saved in health costs, reduced criminality and drug abuse, and in educational, career and financial achievements (Schweinhart *et al.* 1993). While this is a study looking primarily at a specific model of early years education it has relevance for the field of parenting education since a significant element of the programme was parental involvement achieved through parent support via weekly home visits. Since the study High Scope have developed a range of options for parental involvement based on the same philosophy of providing choice with support.

No major long-term research in this field has been conducted in Britain so we are overly reliant on American and some Australian research. The Elmira home visiting study conducted by David Olds was estimated as paying back its costs within four years as a consequence of the substantial savings on reduced use of health care providers and social benefits claims by the mothers and their children (Olds *et al.* 1993, Leventhal 1997). In his comprehensive review of attachment, resilience and prevention Svanberg (1998) notes a small number of support programmes that include a cost benefit analysis element. For example the costs related to child maltreatment and its consequences in Michigan were conservatively assessed and compared to the costs of providing prevention services to all first time parents: for every $1 dollar spent it was estimated that $19 dollars were saved 'further down the line' (Caldwell 1992 cited in Svanberg 1998).

A large study undertaken by the RAND Corporation estimated the number of crimes that would be saved by a $1 million investment in various strategies to tackle delinquents before or after they become chronic offenders. Presented as a cost per household to reduce crime by ten per cent per year, Waller and colleagues estimated that this can be achieved by increasing taxes per household by $228 to pay for prison, or by $118 for delinquent supervision, by $48 to pay for parent training or by $32 for graduation incentives. While funding further education is the greatest cost saving, by opting for parent training as well over incarceration the public are getting between a five- and seven-fold return on their tax dollars with no loss in crime reduction effectiveness (Waller *et al.* 1997)

Using current straight cost comparisons one can see that some integrative programmes (see below) in the UK with robust track records would be worth examining further for their long-term benefits. For example residential care currently costs approximately £1,000 per week. Set this against the approximate costs of: NEWPIN which works with families on the brink of crisis (Jenkins-Hansen 1997) at about £3,600 per family; Pippin working with couples through the transition to parenthood (Parr 1996) at an estimated £560 per couple for their 35 hour course; and the Family Nurturing Network which works with children and their families experiencing behavioural problems at £1,000 per family for a 15 week course (Dean and Klimes 1998).

One intervention programme that offers promising results in providing long-term cost benefit analyses for an integrative model operating at the hard edge of the parenting field is Multi-Systemic Therapy (MST) designed by Scott Henggeler in South Carolina. This is a home and community based services approach using a range of treatment modalities. The pilot programme targeted violent and/or chronic juvenile offenders with serious emotional disturbances. The first focus of MST is to improve psychosocial functioning of the young person and their family. Trained counsellors work with the youth, their family, peer context, school and community/neighbour-hood supports. Each youth is assigned to a therapist who designs individualised interventions following MST principles and according to the needs of the youth and the family. Treatment time in the pilot was three months with a client:therapist ratio of 4:1 at a cost of $3,500. This is set against the average cost of institutional placement in South Carolina of $17,769 per offender. Further to this however at 59 week follow-up, re-arrests and incarcerations were reduced in the study group, families reported increased warmth and cohesion and decreased youth aggression, and positive results were maintained at 2.4 year follow-up with MST doubling the percentage of youth not re-arrested at longer term follow-up (Henggeler *et al.* 1995). Further to these successes programmes working with abusive families and other targeted groups are being tested.

Behaviour modification programmes, as I say above, is by far the easiest form of parenting education to evaluate, and by extension to attach to costings. However, if we are to see *long-term savings* we must seek to examine the more complex, integrative forms of intervention based within communities.

Integration – from prevention to promotion

The benefits of prevention over crisis management, of fences at the top of the cliff over ambulances at the bottom, have long been acknowledged by research and more recently by legislation (see Chapter 1). Preventative approaches are slowly being given a strategic shape within social and health services and integrated into mainstream practice in some geographical areas.

But models of prevention and what one is trying to prevent vary from one professional paradigm to another (see Hardiker *et al.* 1991).

In counterpoint to the 'top down' trend in favour of parent training approaches (as potentially quick fix solutions), discussion is now turning from prevention to promotion, building on the body of evidence from early years education. The Sure Start programme for example is not just about preventing the worst from happening but also about promoting optimal outcomes for children. A promotional model of pro-social parenting education and support seeks to move from the problematisation of family issues to a more prosocial view of parents, children and families; it aims to provide ways of helping parents, families and children avoid coming near the cliff edge in the first place. This model sees learning not as the preserve of 'education' and separate from medical intervention, but as part of a model of healthy living, one that recognises that parents are the child's first teacher.

Thus a promotional perspective addresses such questions as: how do we promote more effective parenting? How can we promote better school readiness in children, better achievement in schools? How do we support the development of resilience in children, parents and families? How do we provide learning opportunities for all families? How do we provide long-term alternatives to offending for young people?

Many of the answers that commentators are providing are based on complex multi-agency work within the community such as the work being done at the Thomas Coram Foundation (Pugh in press) and others described above (see also Barnes 1999).

Open-access programmes based on an Integrative Model, support services within the community, and multi-agency approaches are all far less well evaluated than clinical interventions. Most have developed within the voluntary sector by those with neither the financial means nor often the clinical research training to undertake robust evaluation that can withstand the critical scrutiny of the academic research community. The hegemony of quantitative and comparative analysis (for example randomised controlled trials) over qualitative and subjective analysis (for example parent and child interviews) holds sway despite the many inadequacies of these methods applied to ecological and community situations (Leventhal 1997). This is changing, however, with some leading professionals and academics calling for a reassessment of the status quo (Buchanan 1998). Svanberg (1998) argues for an attachment model for intervention, Stewart-Brown (1998) for considering conduct disorders as part of a spectrum of behaviour and rooted in emotions we should seek to understand, Barnes (1998) for taking a community approach which blends simple practical support solutions with psychological interventions.

For change to impact across a range of measures (e.g. reduction in use of health services and benefits, reduced crime and drug use, raised educational attainment and social involvement) and over the long term (thus yielding the highest savings) interventions, parenting support and learning opportunities must become embedded within people's ways of being and their communities and therefore sustainable by those same communities. Assessing change and benefits accruing from complex, community based models is not straightforward. Research designs must be equally complex, longitudinal and are therefore costly. This requires a major commitment on the part of Government and academics alike to plan for the long term and allocate funds accordingly.

The rise of parenting programmes took off from Keith Joseph's famous reference during the 1970s to the 'cycle of deprivation and despair'. While current policy discussion focuses heavily on the benefits of prevention – of mental and behavioural disorders, of crime, delinquency, drug abuse and teenage pregnancy – we must not lose sight of the vision of those who developed parenting programmes in non-clinical settings, hoping not just to prevent the worst from happening but to enhance parent–child relationships, family life and educational/work achievements – the creation of a cycle of development and hope.

References

Alexander, T. (1998) *Family Learning.* London: DEMOS.
Barlow, J. (1997) *Systematic Review of the Effectiveness of Parent-Training Programmes in Improving the Behaviour of 3–7 Year Old Children.* Oxford, Health Services Research Unit

Barnes, J (1999) *What Works? The Evidence so Far.* Presentation given at a joint CPHVA /PESF conference, 11 February 1999 (available from the Parenting Education & Support Forum).

Bastiani, J. and Wolfendale, S. (1996) *Home–School Work in Britain: review, reflection and development.* London: David Fulton Publishers.

Behr, H. (1997) 'Group work with parents', in Dwivedi, K. (ed.) *Enhancing Parenting Skills, a guide for professionals working with parents.* London: John Wiley.

Bronfenbrenner, U. (1979) *The Ecology of Human Development: experiments by nature and design.* Cambridge: Massachusetts, Harvard University Press.

Buchanan, A. (1998) 'The background', in Buchanan, A. and Hudson, B. (eds) *Parenting, Schooling and Children's Behaviour.* Aldershot: Ashgate Publishing.

Burgess, A. (1997) *Fatherhood Reclaimed: the making of the modern father.* London: Vermilion.

Coleman, J. and Roker, D. (1998) 'Parenting and young people', *The Parenting Forum Newsletter,* Spring 1998.

Cowan, C. P. *et al.* (1991) 'Becoming a family: marriage, parenting and child development' in Cowan, P. A. and Hetherington, M. (eds) *Family Transitions.* London: Lawrence Erlbaum.

Davis, H. and Hester, P. (1996) *An Independent Evaluation of Parent Link, a parenting education programme.* London: Parent Network.

Daws, D. (1989) *Through the Night. Helping parents and sleepless infants.* London: Free Association Books.

Dean, M. and Klimes, I. (1998) 'The Family Connections Project', *Newsletter 83,* February 1998. Leicester: The British Psychological Society Division of Educational and Child Psychology.

DfEE (1997) *Targets for our Future, a consultation document.* London: DfEE.

Downes, P. (1997) 'Crisis time for boys?', *Empowering Parents as Educators. Parenting Forum newsletter,* Autumn.

Einzig, H. (1996) 'Parenting education and support', in Bayne, R. Horton, I. and Bimrose, J. (eds) *New Directions in Counselling.* London: Routledge.

Einzig, H. (1998a) 'The promotion of successful parenting: an agenda for action', in Utting, D. (ed.) *Children's Services, now and in the future.* London: National Children's Bureau.

Einzig, H. (1998b) 'An Overview of Parenting Education and Support'. Presentation at Conference, 11 November 1998. London, Parenting Education & Support Forum.

Einzig, H. and Kordan, L. (1999) Patterns of Parenting Support. Briefing Sheet in Taking Stock and Moving Forward *Parenting Forum Newsletter,* Spring 1999.

Eyre, R. (1997) 'The Under 8's Unit at Marlborough House, Swindon', *Parenting and Crime, The Parenting Forum Briefing Sheet No. 5.* Spring.

Family Links (1997) *The Nurturing Programme in Schools.* Oxford: Family Links, The Office, The Old Rectory, Waterstock, Oxon OX33 1JT.

Fundudis, T. (1997) 'Single parents: risk or resource', *Child Psychology & Psychiatry Review* **2**(1) 2–14.

Gibbons, J. (1991) 'Children in need and their families: outcomes of referrals to social services', *British Journal of Social Work* **21**, 217–27.

Goleman, D. (1996) *Emotional Intelligence.* London: Bloomsbury.

Gottman, D. (1997) *The Heart of Parenting*. London: Bloomsbury.

Greater Shankill Partnership Company Limited (1996) *Early Years Project – Background*. Belfast: Greater Shankill Partnership Company Limited.

Grimshaw, R. and McGuire, C. (1998) *Evaluating Parenting Programmes: a study of stakeholders' views*. London: National Children's Bureau.

Hardiker, P., Exton, K. and Barker, M. 'The social policy contexts of prevention in child care', *British Journal of Social Work*, **21**(4) 341–59.

Henggeler, S., Schoenwald, S. K., Pickrel, S. G. (1995) 'Multisystemic therapy: bridging the gap between university and community-based treatment'. *Journal of Consulting & Clinical Psychology*, **63** (5), 709–17.

Home Office (1998a) *Boys, Young Men and Fathers*. Report of a ministerial seminar 16 November 1998. London: Home Office.

Home Office (1998b) *Crime and Disorder Act*. London: Home Office.

Howell, E., Montuschi, O., Kahn, T. (1997) *Parenting Perspectives: a guide to teaching parenting skills*. Bury St. Edmunds: Courseware Publications.

Janis-Norton, N. (1997) *The New Learning Centre: skills for success at school and harmony in the home*. London: New Learning Centre.

Jenkins-Hansen, A. (1997) *National NEWPIN*. London: National NEWPIN.

Kordan, L (1999) *Patterns of Parenting Support: three case studies*. London: Mental Health Foundation.

Kraemer, S. (1997) 'Parenting, childcare and early attachments', *Parenting Forum Newsletter No. 7*, Summer 1997.

Kraemer, S. (1998) *Resilience and Attachment*. Tavistock Clinic Paper. London: Tavistock Clinic.

Leventhal, J. (1997) 'The prevention of child abuse and neglect: pipe dreams or possibilities?', *Clinical Child Psychology and Psychiatry* **2**(4): 489–500. Sage.

Lloyd, E., *et al.* (1997) *Today and Tomorrow: investing in our children*. Barkingside: Barnardo's.

Lloyd, E. (ed.) (1999) *What Works in Parenting Education*. Barkingside: Barnardo's.

Long, N. (1997) 'Parent education/training in the USA: current status and future trends', *Clinical Child Psychology and Psychiatry* **2**(4) 501–15. Sage.

Makins, V. (1997) *Not Just a Nursery. Multi-agency early years centres in action*. London: National Children's Bureau.

Mental Health Foundation (1999) *The Big Picture: national inquiry into the mental health of children and young people*. London: Mental Health Foundation.

Murphy, E. (1996) 'Working with teenage fathers in prison', *The Parenting Forum Newsletter*, No. 4, Autumn 1996.

Olds, D. L., *et al.* (1993) 'Effect of prenatal and infancy nurse home visitation on government spending', *Medical Care* **31**, 155–74. USA.

Parenting Education & Support Forum (1996, 1997a) *Constitution*. London: Parenting Education & Support Forum.

Parenting Education & Support Forum (1997b) *Membership Flyer*. London: Parenting Education & Support Forum.

Parr, M. (1996) 'Support for Couples in the Transition to Parenthood', Ph.D. Evaluation Report of the Development of PIPPIN's Parent–Infant Programme. London, University of East London.

Phillips, A. (1993) *The Trouble with Boys, Parenting the Men of the Future.* London: Pandora.

Pinder, R. (1999) 'Rotherham parents speak', 'Taking stock – looking to the future', *Parenting Forum Newsletter 14*, Spring 1999.

Pitt, J. (1998) 'Parenting teenagers courses in rural North Yorkshire', *The Parenting Forum Newsletter, 10*, Spring 1998.

Play Council (1998) *Home Zones.* London: Play Council

Pound, A. and Mills, M. (1985) 'A pilot evaluation of NEWPIN, a home-visiting and befriending scheme in South London', *ACPP Newsletter* **7**(4).

Puckering, C. *et al.* (1994) 'Process and evaluation of a group intervention for mothers with parenting difficulties'. *Child Abuse Review* **3** 299–310.

Pugh, G., De'Ath, E., Smith, C. (1994) *Confident Parents, Confident Children.* London: National Children's Bureau.

Pugh, G. (in press). 'Young children and their families: creating a community response', in Abbott, L. and Moylett, H. (eds), *Early Education Re-formed.* London: Falmer Press.

Rutter, M. (1974) 'Dimensions of parenthood: some myths and some suggestions', *The Family in Society, Dimensions of Parenthood.* London: HMSO.

Schweinhart, L., Barnes, H. and Weikart, D. (1993) *Significant Benefits: the High/Scope Perry Pre-school Study through age 27.* Ypsilanti, Michigan: High Scope Press.

Shinman, S. (1994) *Family Album: snapshots of home start in words and pictures.* Leicester: Home Start UK.

Smith, C. (1996) *Developing Parenting Programmes.* London: National Children's Bureau.

Smith, C. and Pugh, G. (1996) *Learning to be a Parent, a survey of group based parenting programmes.* London: Family Policy Studies Centre.

Steele, M. (1997) 'Intergenerational cycles of attachment: recent advances in research on parenting', *Parenting, Child Care and Early Attachments. Parenting Forum Newsletter No. 7*, Summer 1997.

Stewart-Brown, S. (1998) 'Public health implications of childhood behaviour problems and parenting programmes', in Buchanan, A. and Hudson, B., *Parenting, Schooling and Children's Behaviour.* Aldershot: Ashgate Publishing.

Svanberg, Per O. G. (1998) 'Attachment, resilience and prevention', *Journal of Mental Health* **7**(6), 543–78.

Utting, D. (1997) 'Parenting and crime', *Parenting and Society. Parenting Forum Newsletter No. 6* Briefing Sheet No. 5. London: Parenting Education & Support Forum.

Utting, D., Bright, J. Henricson, C. (1993) *Crime and the Family, Improving Child-rearing and Preventing Delinquency.* London: Family Policy Studies Centre.

Waller, I., Welsh, B. and Sansfacon, D. (1997) *Crime Prevention Digest 1997.* Montreal, International Centre for the Prevention of Crime.

Webster-Stratton, C. (1997) 'From parent training to community building', *Families in Society, the Journal of Contemporary Human Services*, **78**(2), 156–71.

Webster-Stratton, C. (1999) 'Researching the impact of parent training programmes on child conduct disorder', in Lloyd, E. *et al.* (eds) *What Works in Parenting Education.* Barkingside: Barnardos.

Webster-Stratton, C. and Taylor, T. K. (1998) 'Adopting and implementing empirically supported interventions: a recipe for success', in Buchanan, A. and Hudson, B. (eds) *Parenting, Schooling and Children's Behaviour.* Aldershot: Ashgate Publishing.

Chapter 3

Families and society: change and continuity

Janet Walker

> Families are at the heart of our society... Our future depends on their success in bringing up children... (*Supporting Families: A Consultation Document, 1998*)

Towards the end of 1998, the Government published a consultation paper on the family, marking the beginning of a debate and setting out 'a major programme of action'. The Home Secretary described the paper as being about 'the practical support the government can provide to help parents do the best they can for their children' (*Supporting Families: A Consultation Document*, 1998). It acknowledges that families are under stress, that family structures have become more complex, and that a modern family policy needs to recognise these new realities. This chapter considers the nature and impact of some of these new realities.

The centrality of family life

Throughout history people have sought to establish an ideal human community in which both physical and emotional needs are met. Generally speaking, the family unit has been regarded as the best source of support and care for children, the sick and the elderly, and as the vital means whereby cultural values and responsibilities are preserved and passed on to the next generation. Usually, it is within the family that children first learn to communicate, and are nurtured, socialised and prepared for adult life (Walker 1995a). Parents are key, but are not necessarily the only players in these activities. While family functions are universal, there is no particular universal structure in which these are carried out (Ishwaran 1989). Families and societies are always changing and evolving. Relationships and responsibilities are continuously being modified throughout the life-course as a result both of time and ageing and of social and economic circumstances (Allan 1999). In the twentieth century, however, it is the sheer pace of change that has had an unparalleled impact on family organisation, living arrangements and personal relationships.

People today in the western world experience the enormous opportunities and freedoms that are associated with living in the age of the global village, and of rapid technological advance which has resulted in widespread access to a universe of virtual reality via the internet, health care which can provide replacements for almost every part of the body, and education programmes which go well beyond childhood and into the third age. But new opportunities bring new challenges, while many long-standing problems such as social exclusion, discrimination, poverty, unemployment and the fear and impact of crime and abuse persist as major social pressures, all of which threaten the stability of family life. In recent years, governments have become concerned that the risks for individuals and for society are now too high, and so have begun to look for new ways of buttressing, supporting and protecting family relationships, most notably those between parents and children.

Most people in the UK live in families, but fewer than half live in what is commonly described as the 'traditional' family containing a married couple with their biological children. Most children live with both parents (who may not be married), but there has been a substantial increase in the number of lone parent families over the last 25 years (ONS 1997). Lone parent households are not recent constructions in terms of family living arrangements. In the mid-1990s about one in five children under the age of 15 lived with a lone parent, as against one in eight in the 1850s, but if we add to those the children in Victorian England who were in institutional care, and those who lived with other relatives, then the proportion of children being brought up outside the two-parent family unit 150 years ago was much the same as it is now (Anderson 1994). Society's expectations of parents, however, are much greater than ever before, and the pressures on lone parents are considerable.

Changing family dynamics

Contraception has provided women with greater choice in relation to child-bearing, and higher education has provided them with far more career opportunities (ONS 1997). Although most women have children at some stage in their lives, they are increasingly deferring parenthood until they are in their thirties, and are having fewer children. Since the early beginnings of capitalism the man has been expected to be the head of the household and the family breadwinner. Historically, women have been largely economically dependent on men. This has changed, and by the early 1990s over 60 per cent of married mothers and some 40 per cent of lone mothers were in employment (OPCS 1994). By 1996, women represented 44 per cent of the labour force of working age. Whereas in the early 1980s husbands were the sole income-earner in 40 per cent of households, by the mid-1990s this percentage had fallen to just over 25 per cent. Never before have so many women and mothers with young children been employed outside the home. Although mothers with children under five are the least likely to be in paid employment, it is this group of women who have experienced the greatest increase in labour market participation in the last ten years (ONS 1997). Not surprisingly, when both partners work outside the home traditional gender roles within the family are challenged, yet it is the more traditional division of labour which continues to provide a template against which parents are judged. A model of partnership in which paternal and maternal roles are delineated, clearly defined and complementary continues to evoke a powerful image of stability and permanence (Walker 1996).

As we enter a new millennium, there is a continuing struggle between the old and the new. There has been a dramatic shift away from a model of partnership which is based on social and economic considerations to one based on a companionate relationship from which personal, emotional benefits are derived. People want and expect more from their family relationships, and the increasing emphasis on personal fulfilment and individualism in the 1980s and 1990s has changed the way in which they view and form partnerships and approach parenthood. Young people are much more likely to postpone marriage in favour of living with one, or several, partners as cohabitants (Kiernan and Estaugh 1993). At the beginning of the twenty-first century some 80 per cent of marrying couples will have cohabited, compared with just 25 per cent in the 1960s. Like lone parenthood, cohabitation is not new: before legal marriage became widely adopted in the nineteenth century, many couples opted to live together claiming some status through 'common law'. It has been estimated that between 1750 and 1850, as much as 20 per cent of the population of England and Wales cohabited for a time (Gillis 1985). What has changed, however, is couples cohabiting as a stage in the process of partnering and as a prelude to marriage. Whereas in 1966 only four per cent of women who married for the first time had lived with their husband beforehand, in 1993 68 per cent had done so. There has also been a shift towards people cohabiting for longer periods, associated with a decline in the number of people getting married. Between 1971 and 1993 the rate of first marriages decreased more than 50 per cent. Most couples begin married life having experienced earlier sexual relationships, and increasing numbers have already become parents. The charity Childline has reported increasing numbers of calls from children aged between 10 and 14 who fear they might be pregnant. Teenage mothers experience severe pressures when they become parents.

Over a third of all live births are outside marriage, which is more than four times the same proportion in the 1970s, but most of the parents are living together and some 80 per cent of births to single women are jointly registered by both parents. It has been suggested (Boh 1989) that one of the main contradictions inherent in family life today relates to the increased freedom of conjugal choice on the one hand and the constraints bound up with parenthood on the other. Parenthood requires no specific form of family structure, yet, in our society at least, the process of becoming a parent has traditionally been associated with being in a marital relationship. Furthermore, family structures in most cultures have been based on some form of monogamous marriage, a committed adult relationship for life which conforms to an image of what constitutes stability. Edgar (1993) has commented that the most profound change in family life over recent decades is that the meaning of parenthood is being transformed in concert with the reconstruction of marital relationships.

As women have sought and achieved greater gender equality in almost all aspects of daily life, their expectations regarding marriage have changed substantially. No longer are they prepared to be dependent on their husbands socially and economically, nor are they willing to suffer in silence when they find themselves in abusive relationships. Marriage is increasingly viewed as an equal partnership in which tasks and responsibilities are to be shared. Many couples achieve this, but it is clear that the arrival of children inevitably alters the couple relationship and seems to reassert traditional gender roles. Even the 'new' man is unlikely to play an equal part in parenting tasks. Women, on the other hand, often struggle to combine and balance work and home commitments, managing childcare as part of a complex array of responsibilities. Many are unprepared for this apparent shift towards traditional roles, and conflict within the marriage is not uncommon. Research by Mansfield *et al.* (1996) found that couples who had successfully managed the transition to parenthood either already had differentiated roles or else had effectively renegotiated their partnerships to accommodate the demands of children.

The quest for personal fulfilment

In a culture which subscribes to people doing what is personally satisfying and which values 'getting ahead', people find themselves caught between opposing sets of values: those which uphold the sanctity of marriage and the virtues of family life, and those which emphasise individualism and personal achievement. Tellingly, a series of Gallup polls conducted in the United States between the 1970s and 1990s revealed that nine out of ten people would welcome more emphasis on traditional family ties (Hugick and Leonard 1991). Modern marriage, according to Giddens (1991), is not anchored in the external conditions of social-economic life, but is focused on intimacy. Marriage endures, therefore, only if it continues to provide emotional satisfaction. When, in 1994, a sample of people in Great Britain were asked if they thought that discontented couples should stay together for the sake of the children, only 20 per cent of respondents thought that they should (ONS 1997). Giddens (1996) talks of the 'de-traditionalisation' of marriage: tradition no longer provides order and meaning, and marriage has become one of a number of ways of constructing family relationships. This implies a greater freedom of individual choice, although this alone does not necessarily imply any rejection of responsibility. Reynolds and Mansfield (1999) conceptualise individualism as a continuum. At one extreme, individualism stresses not only individuals' rights but also their obligations; this may be termed 'moral individualism'. At the other extreme, individualism stresses personal autonomy above the needs of others, which may be termed pragmatic individualism (Simons 1995). On the one hand, then, family life is valued for the meaning it gives to individual lives, while on the other it is valued as a means to self-fulfilment.

A major concern is that the shift from moral to pragmatic individualism is incompatible with notions of the family and will lead to even greater diversity in family forms. Reviewing the evidence, Reynolds and Mansfield (1999) conclude that while evidence of individualism is strong, and while the concept of marriage continues to change, family relationships are being revised rather than rejected (Bumpass 1990; Popenoe 1993). Although women and men tend to agree on the importance of emotional support and companionship in marriage, women, it seems, are more likely to be disappointed. A study of marital instability in the United States has found that women in the 1980s who adopted less traditional attitudes towards gender roles experienced a decline in the quality of their marriages and were more likely to divorce. Significantly, husbands who adopted less traditional attitudes experienced a better quality of marriage, though they were also prone to divorce (Amato and Booth 1995).

The number of marriages in the UK ending in divorce more than trebled between 1969 and 1994. It is anticipated that some 40 per cent of marriages will continue to be dissolved each year, and that some 70 per cent of these will involve children under the age of 16. Divorce has become more socially acceptable, and it has become easier for people to justify terminating their marriage (Eurobarometer 1993). When communication has broken down common interests no longer exist, and when 'love' is not mutual divorce becomes a 'rational' solution (Reynolds and Mansfield 1999), yet divorce is a topic which continues to arouse concern and controversy. Almost no other issue save that of capital punishment elicits such public attention and provokes such strongly opposed reactions (Walker and Hornick 1996).

The best interests of children

Despite more liberal attitudes towards divorce, there are many potentially detrimental consequences. The presence of children in the home is a factor which those considering separation or divorce take seriously, and some of them do decide to stay together for the sake of the children even when the marriage is an empty shell. It is the impact of divorce on children which has caused the most public concern in recent years. During the passage of the Family Law Bill through Parliament in 1996, children were the focus of much attention. Lord Jakobovits, for example, referred to 'tens of thousands of children who might be crippled for the rest of their life' (*Hansard*, 23 January 1996). Divorce, however, like other aspects of family life is not a new phenomenon. Ancient civilisations sanctioned it, although husbands had more rights to divorce than wives. The highly restrictive moral code of medieval canon law made divorce virtually impossible, except for the rich and powerful who could lobby and bribe their way to annulments from Rome. Historical data demonstrate that unhappy couples tended nevertheless to lead separate lives, or to enter into extra-marital liaisons, producing illegitimate children who had few rights and often little family stability. The majority of marriages were terminated only through the death of a spouse. Lower life-expectancy meant that, in the 1850s, as many marriages were terminated in the first 15 years by death as in the 1980s were ended through divorce. The difference for children, however, is that death renders the loss of a parent absolute, whereas divorce represents only a partial loss for most children, but the impact of uncertainty surrounding contact can be devastating, particularly in the short term.

Divorce is almost always stressful, resulting in intense feelings of grief, sadness, rejection, anger, bitterness and hostility, and an overwhelming sense of loss for everyone involved. Marriages disintegrate over time, and it is now widely accepted that the separation and divorce of parents 'is not a single event in the lives of children. It is a process which begins, for many, years before the divorce, and has repercussions that reverberate into adulthood' (Kiernan 1991, p.4). There is abundant evidence that marital conflict can have damaging effects for children, but it must be remembered that

> the fact that a young person comes from a divorced family does not, in itself, tell us a great deal about how he or she is faring or embarking into adulthood. While the effects of divorce are very real, they are not inevitable, and should not be exaggerated – a balanced view is needed. (Zill 1996, p.25)

In assessing the consequences for children, a number of factors must be taken into account. These include the way in which children are prepared for divorce (most are not); arrangements for continued parenting and contact with each parent; day-to-day living arrangements; the number of disruptions and transitions; and, most critically, the quality of the relationships between all those involved (Walker 1996). Children are seen as the innocent victims, and much media and political attention has been focused on their fate.

In order to achieve a better sense of balance here the Joseph Rowntree Foundation commissioned a detailed review of all recent research into the consequences for children of marital breakdown. Having considered over 200 research reports, Rodgers and Pryor (1998) concluded that children whose parents split up have about twice the likelihood of experiencing specific poor outcomes in the long term as those in intact families. There is a higher probability of children from separated families being in poverty and poor housing; being poorer as adults; having behavioural problems; performing less well at school; needing medical treatment; leaving school/home when young; becoming sexually active, pregnant or a parent at a young age; having depressive symptoms; and exhibiting high levels of smoking, drinking and drug use during adolescence and adulthood. Rodgers and Pryor list the factors affecting the outcomes for children as financial hardship, family conflict (before, during and after separation), parental ability to recover from the distress of marital breakdown, multiple changes in family structure, and the quality of contact with the non-resident parent. Equally importantly, their review found that the absence of a parent is not the most important factor affecting child development, that the age at which children experience separation is not in itself important, and that boys are not more adversely affected than girls.

There is no doubt, however, that divorce does have profound effects on parenting. The stress of marital breakdown can result in poorer physical and mental health for parents. Some parents may turn to alcohol, and financial hardship can cause serious disadvantage and social exclusion. Our research over the past 15 years has revealed that as financial pressures bite, resentment increases, communication becomes strained and conflict flourishes – just the kind of conditions which undermine parenting abilities and cause the greatest difficulties for children (McCarthy et al. 1991). Indeed, conflict-ridden families, whatever their composition or marital status, create the most difficult environment for the well-being of children. Certainly the most distressed children are those who become pawns in their parents' battles.

Unclear families

A recent meta-analysis of 65 families found a consistent link between the quality of the marriage and the quality of parenting (Erel and Burman 1995). It is reasonable to suppose that the link between the quality of the parents' relationship and the quality of the parenting will hold good in respect of non-married, cohabiting parents and for those who have divorced. Preliminary findings from a Californian study suggest that offering parents support to improve the quality of their relationship with each other has more impact on their children's behaviour and performance at kindergarten than teaching specific parenting skills (Cowan and Cowan 1998, reported in Simons 1999).

One of the most far-reaching consequences of marriage breakdown is the lack of clarity about roles and responsibilities, particularly in respect of parenting. Relationships between parents who no longer share an intimate loving relationship as a couple are extremely vulnerable. Research shows that these parents frequently have to surmount major obstacles in their endeavour to share parental responsibilities in a climate of mutual respect and trust (Simpson 1998; Simpson *et al.* 1995). The sad fact is that the incompatibility which contributes to the relationship failing often continues in the experience of parenting. Popular wisdom would have us believe that a significant proportion of fathers drop out of their children's lives after divorce, abandoning their parental responsibilities. The reality for many children after divorce is that fathers come to occupy a decidedly secondary parental position in comparison to mothers, a position which usually has to be negotiated with caution, and which may well be rather precarious. For men especially, divorce represents a major disjunction in the life cycle. Post-divorce parenting, particularly when conducted from a distance, is far from easy or straightforward. Becoming a 'subsidiary' parent, as Schaffer (1990) has described it, with limited contact under artificial conditions is not conducive to maintaining a close parental relationship. Fathers describe becoming more like an uncle or friend to their children, and less like a parent (Simpson *et al.* 1995). The losses for everyone concerned can be considerable, and parental relationships that are conducted against a backdrop of anger, frustration and discontent are inevitably impoverished. There are no easy solutions to the question of how the care of and responsibility for children should be shared between parents who do not live together, yet children derive real benefits – psychological, social and economic – when divorced parents can work together in the upbringing of their children (Cummings and Davies 1994). If they cannot, effective contact with the non-resident parent becomes considerably more difficult and stressful. Staying in touch with children is also heavily influenced by external factors such as finance, housing, transport and employment. Poorer, and unemployed, fathers appear to be more likely to drop out of their children's lives. Furthermore, the relationship between a father and his children after divorce is shaped and redefined in the context of other crucial relationships in the wider kin system, most specifically by the emergence of step-relationships.

Parental roles and responsibilities may become even more unclear when a child has a stepmother or stepfather. These new family constructions bring new complexities into family dynamics as new relationships have to be integrated with new forms of old relationships (Simpson 1994). Becoming a parent to someone else's children is a difficult challenge, and can make enormous demands on the parenting skills of a new partner, which may feel overwhelming. Divorced parents are rarely prepared for the fundamental emotional, psychological and practical changes which have to be accommodated. What is clear is that the quality of one relationship can affect all the others.

Parents in the middle

Divorce fragments families, and children may not only lose touch with one of their parents, but may also find themselves disconnected from other kin, particularly grandparents. Our own research with three-generational families around the UK demonstrates the importance of grandparenting not only for children but for grandparents themselves (Anderson *et al.*, in preparation). It is predicted that by the year 2021 nearly 20 per cent of the UK population will be over 65. By 2031 the number of people of pensionable age, many of whom will be over 85, will exceed 16 million, more than double the number in 1961 (CSO 1994). By contrast, by 2031 the proportion of children under 16 is expected to fall to 18 per cent of the population.

While the growing elderly population can be viewed as highly positive for society and for families, one current reality is that women may find themselves in a continuous 'cycle of caring' over the life-course (Graham 1991). This can be a source of continuing unease for the elderly, and of inter-generational conflict within families, and can be an added pressure on adult children who are themselves struggling to cope with parenting responsibilities. Moreover, the implications of divorce and remarriage for the family lives of older people are considerable: there may be four or more sets of elderly grandparents in need of care and support, some of whom are cut off from their children and grandchildren.

The challenge of parenting

A number of studies have drawn attention to the link between parental supervision, discipline and delinquency, and have suggested that good parenting protects against the acquisition of a criminal record (Utting *et al.* 1993). With crime rates having risen during the last 25 years, parents are being made to face up to the misdemeanours of their children and may find themselves subject to a Parenting Order compelling them to attend a course on parenting (Section 8, Crime and Disorder Act 1998). The critical input of both parents into a child's development and into early learning is, according to Ball (1994), self-evident, but has frequently been ignored. During the 1990s, increasing numbers of children have run away from home, and the most common reasons they give for this are violence and abuse, not being listened to, and not being cared about (Stein *et al.* 1994). Few of these children speak positively about family life. A report on street children in Europe commissioned in 1992 highlighted the significance of divorce, poor parenting, economic hardship, abuse and neglect as common causes of homelessness among children. It concluded that there must be investment in primary support for families (Brown 1994).

The latest projections indicate that by the year 2021 the married population will be the minority, while cohabitation will continue to increase (Population Trends 1999). The centrality of parenting as one of the most challenging and important tasks of adulthood is not in doubt. Parents who separate are not absolved from their responsibilities, but parenting in these circumstances demands a good deal of work and commitment as relationships are reconstructed. Diversity in family structures is not in itself a problem, nor are departures from the 'traditional' family necessarily harmful to children, but the notion of continuity is central – continuity in care, in relationships, in support. It is discontinuity, not diversity, which is hazardous (Walker 1995b). Modern parenthood is demanding and complex and not everyone has the essential skills to manage it well.

Supporting families

In a fast-moving busy world there are many pressures on parents. These may be linked to adverse economic circumstances such as unemployment, low income or lone parenthood; or they may result from over-demanding jobs, long working hours, or caring for elderly relatives. Expectations surrounding parenting are high, but preparation for it may be woefully inadequate. Unhappy parents do not provide a good environment for children, hence the growing belief that working with families and parents to support them in the task of bringing up children is worthwhile (Newman and Roberts 1999). The All Party Parliamentary Group on Parenting acknowledged in its report during the International Year of the Family in 1994 that all families need help with the normal problems that occur from time to time. It recommended, among other things, that information on relationships, families and parenting, and on where to go for help, should be more widely available and that voluntary sector organisations providing parenting education should be better resourced.

Despite a burgeoning of parent education programmes in recent years, Smith (1996) has estimated that only about four per cent of the parenting population have attended. Two of the key policy questions are whether such programmes should be preventative or remedial (or both), and whether there should be compulsion to attend, particularly when parents separate or get divorced. Einzig (1998) has argued that universally available parenting programmes should be targeted around the major transitions in family life such as the birth of a child. Divorce is clearly an obvious transition to target, and mandatory programmes are being extended across the United States and in Canada. Evaluations of such programmes are just beginning to emerge. The majority of parents indicate that they have appreciated the opportunity to attend, and that they believe that as a result they are being more cooperative as parents and relating more effectively with their children (McKenzie and Guberman 1996).

The new government proposals for supporting families include a wide variety of measures such as helplines, improved practical support, promotion of family-friendly employment practice, support for problems such as youth offending and teenage pregnancy, and interventions to strengthen marriage and promote continuing parenting after divorce. A legislative framework for some of these ideas is already in place. The Family Law Act 1996 heralds a new approach to the legal dissolution of marriage. It aims to support marriage wherever possible, and to ensure that people considering divorce have full information about the options available to them. It has been described as one of the most radical and far-reaching reforms of family justice in the twentieth century.

Before the divorce process can begin in any formal, legal sense, anyone who wishes to start the process will have to attend an information meeting at least three months before making a statement of marital breakdown. Information will be given on a wide range of topics, including how the parents may acquire a better understanding of the ways in which children can be helped to cope with the breakdown of their parents' marriage. In this sense the Act is conceptually unusual in that it seeks to promote a collaboration between the legal process and various interventions intended to minimise the damage done to children and adults (Cretney and Masson 1997). Since June 1997 some 14 pilot projects, covering 11 areas of England and Wales, have been testing different models of providing the information (Walker 1999, a and b). The information pack includes a Parenting Plan designed to encourage parents to focus on the needs of their children and plan for the future in practical everyday ways. The Plan consists of a small booklet entitled *Planning for Your Children's Future*, which gives information about the needs of children and provides a pro-forma in which parents can record the arrangements they are making for their children, under nine broad headings (Richards *et al.* 1999). The completed document is not enforceable by the court, but it may provide a blueprint for parents to negotiate and share parental tasks and responsibilities. Parenting Plans are widely used in North America, and are currently being piloted in New Zealand and Canada. The Plans are not only practical, but also educational, and have been welcomed by professionals and parents alike. It seems clear from the preliminary data from the information meeting pilots that the Parenting Plan is providing focus and clarity in respect of what issues need to be considered and the problems which can arise in the future. It may also help parents to begin the difficult and demanding process of renegotiation of new patterns of parenting relationships. Given the increasing number of children involved in the break-up of cohabiting relationships the question must be asked regarding whether information meetings should in some way be mandatory for them also. A number of recent studies have identified the information needs of parents as health and healthcare, child development, schooling, children's behaviour and careers guidance. Groups such as lone parents have particular information needs for themselves as well as for their children. Fathers ask in particular for childcare information and information on children's health (Nicholas and Marden 1997; Roberts *et al.* 1996).

The many changes that have taken place in family life over the last half-century have resulted in a plethora of arrangements for the organisation of domestic and intimate relationships in which the configurations of gender, space and time are highly variable (Simpson 1998). Continuities and discontinuities both in family life and in society pave the way for new discourses and new directions.

References

Allan, G. (ed.) (1999) *The Sociology of the Family.* Oxford: Blackwell.

Amato, P. and Booth, A. (1995) 'Change in gender – role attitudes and perceived marital quality', *American Sociological Review* **60**, 58–66.

Anderson, M. (1994) 'Today's families in historical context', Joseph Rowntree Foundation Family and Parenthood Seminar Paper.

Anderson, M., Tunaley, J., Walker, J. (in preparation) *Communication in Three-Generational Families.*

Ball, Sir C. (1994) 'Start right: the importance of early learning', *The Journal of the Royal Society for the Encouragement of Arts, Manufactures and Commerce.*

Boh, K. (1989) 'European family life patterns – a reappraisal', in Boh, K. *et al.* (eds) *Changing Patterns of European Family Life.* London: Routledge.

Brown, G. (1994) 'The streets of Europe', in *Children in Focus.* London: The Children's Society.

Bumpass, L. (1990) 'What's happening to the family? Interactions between demographic and institutional changes', *Demography* **27**, 483–98.

Central Statistical Office (CSO) (1994) *Social Trends 24.* London: HMSO.

Cretney, S. M. and Masson, J. M. (1997) *Principles of Family Law,* 6th edn. London: Sweet & Maxwell.

Cummings, E. M. and Davies, P. (1994) *Children and Marital Conflict: the impact of family dispute and resolution.* New York: Guilford Press.

Edgar, D. (1993) *Parents at the Core of Family Life: family matters.* Melbourne: Australian Institute of Family Studies.

Einzig, H. (1998) 'The promotion of successful parenting: an agenda for action', in Utting, D. (ed.) *Children's Services: now and in the future.* London: National Children's Bureau.

Erel, O. and Burman, B. (1995) 'Interrelatedness of marital relations and parent–child relations: a meta-analytic review', *Psychological Bulletin* **118**, 108–32.

Eurobarometer (1993) 'Les Europeans et la famille', *Eurobarometre* **39**. (Brussels: EU.)

Giddens, A. (1991) *Modernity and Self-identity.* Cambridge: Polity Press.

Giddens, A. (1996) *In Defence of Sociology: Essays, interpretations and rejoinders.* Cambridge: Polity Press.

Gillis, J. R. (1985) *For Better, for Worse: British marriages, 1600 to the present.* Oxford: Oxford University Press.

Graham, H. (1991) 'The informal sector of welfare: a crisis in caring', *Social Science and Medicine* **32**, 507–15.

Home Office (1998) Crime and Disorder Act (c.37). London: Stationery Office.

Hugick, L. and Leonard, J. (1991) 'Sex in America', *Gallup Poll Monthly* **313**, 60–73.

Ishwaran, K. (1989) *Family and Marriage: cross-cultural perspectives.* Toronto: Wall & Thompson.

Kiernan, K. E. (1991) 'What about the children?', *Family Policy Bulletin,* December (Family Policy Studies Centre).

Kiernan, K. E. and Estaugh, V. (1993) *Cohabitation, Extra-marital Child Bearing and Social Policy.* Occasional Paper No. 17. London: Family Policy Studies Centre.

McCarthy, P., Simpson, R., Walker, J., Corlyon, J. (1991) 'Longitudinal study of the different dispute resolution processes on post-divorce relationships between parents and children', *Report to the Fund for Research in Dispute Resolution.* Newcastle upon Tyne: University of Newcastle.

McKenzie, B. and Guberman, I. (1996) *For the Sake of the Children: a parent education program for separating and divorcing parents.* University of Manitoba: Child and Family Services Research Group.

Mansfield, P., Collard, J., McAllister, F. (1996) *Person, Partner, Parent.* London: Macmillan.

Newman, T. and Roberts, H. (1999) 'Assessing effectiveness', in Lloyd, E. *What Works in Parenting Education.* London: Barnardo's.

Nicholas, D. and Marden N. (1997) *The Information Needs of Parents: case study: parents of children under the age of five.* British Library Research and Innovation Report 56. London: British Library Research and Innovation Centre.

Office for National Statistics (ONS) (1997) *Social Focus on Families.* London: Stationery Office.

OPCS (1994) *General Household Survey.* London: HMSO.

Popenoe, D. (1993) 'American family decline 1960–1990: a review and appraisal', *Journal of Marriage and the Family* **55**(3), 527–42.

Report of the All Party Parliamentary Group on Parenting and International Year of the Family UK: Parliamentary Hearings (1994). London: Tynehart.

Reynolds, J. and Mansfield, P. (1999) 'The effect of changing attitudes to marriage on its stability', in Simons, J. (ed.) *High Divorce Rates: The state of the evidence on reasons and remedies.* Research Series No. 2/99 (vol. 1). London: Lord Chancellor's Department.

Richards, M., Connell, J., Kain, J., Laing, K. (1999) 'Parenting plans', in Walker, J. (ed.) (1999) *Information Meetings and Associated Provisions within the Family Law Act: Third Interim Report to the Lord Chancellor's Department.* University of Newcastle upon Tyne: Newcastle Centre for Family Studies [restricted policy].

Roberts, C., Cronin, N., Dodd, T. (1996) *Parenting Problems: a national study of parents and parenting problems.* London: Family Policy Studies Centre/OPCS.

Rodgers, B. and Pryor, J. (1998) *Divorce and Separation: the outcomes for children.* York: Joseph Rowntree Foundation.

Schaffer, R. (1990) *Making Decisions about Children: psychological questions and answers.* Oxford: Blackwell.

Simons, J. (1995) 'Fertility and values in 15 Western countries during the 1980s', in de Moor, R. (ed.) *Values in Western Societies.* Tilburg: Tilburg University Press.

Simons, J. (1999) 'Can marriage preparation courses influence the quality and stability of family life?', in Simons, J. (ed.) *High Divorce Rates: the state of the evidence on reasons and remedies.* Research Series No. 2/99 (vol. 1). London: Lord Chancellor's Department.

Simpson, B. (1994) 'Bringing the unclear family into focus: divorce and remarriage in contemporary Britain', *Man* (n.s.) **29**, 831–51.

Simpson, B. (1998) *Changing Families.* Oxford: Berg.

Simpson, B., McCarthy, P., Walker, J. (1995) *Being There: fathers after divorce.* University of Newcastle upon Tyne: Relate Centre for Family Studies.

Smith, C. (1996) *Developing Parenting Programmes.* London: National Children's Bureau.

Stein, M., Frost, N., Rees, G. (1994) *Running the Risk: young people in the streets of Britain today.* London: The Children's Society.

Supporting Families: a consultation document (1998). London: Stationery Office.

Utting, D., Bright, J., Henricson, C. (1993) *Crime and the Family: Improving child rearing and preventing delinquency.* London: Family Policy Studies Centre.

Walker, J. (1995a) *The Cost of Communication Breakdown.* London: British Telecom.

Walker, J. (1995b) 'Parenting in the 1990s: great expectations and hard times', *RSA Journal* **143** (5,456), 29–42.

Walker, J. (1996) 'Partnership and parenthood', in Davies, M. (ed.) *The Blackwell Companion to Social Work*, 103–110. London: Cavendish.

Walker, J. (ed.) (1999a) *Information Meetings and Associated Provisions within the Family Law Act: Third Interim Evaluation Report to the Lord Chancellor's Department.* University of Newcastle upon Tyne: Newcastle Centre for Family Studies [restricted policy].

Walker, J. (1999b) *Information Meetings and Associated Provisions within the Family Law Act: Summary of Research in Progress.* London: Lord Chancellor.

Walker, J. and Hornick, J. P. (1996) *Communication in Marriage and Divorce: A Consultation on family law.* London: The BT Forum.

Zill, N. (1996) quoted in Walker, J. and Hornick, J. P., *Communication in Marriage and Divorce: a consultation on family law.* London: The BT Forum.

Chapter 4

_____

Parents as key determinants in planning and delivering parenting education and support programmes: an inclusive ideology

Sheila Wolfendale

Introduction

One key message pervades this chapter – it is that parents ought to be entitled to participate directly in planning and delivering parenting education and support programmes as an active expression of partnership and as part of quality assurance and accountability. It would be ironic if an intervention area that promotes partnership did not also practise it.

This chapter will explore the dimensions and potential of parents as 'equal determinants' of service delivery. There has been more work and therefore more examples of this form of expression of partnership in spheres such as education and survey research, to cite but two, than yet obtains within parenting education and support programmes. So a number of these other initiatives will be referred to, to ascertain parallels between related areas; to see what 'lessons' can be learned from prior experience; how applicable other exemplars are to the specific intervention area of parenting education and support.

It is part of the remit of the chapter to then go on to attempt to construct and offer a model for involving parents as partners in planning and delivering parenting education which is premised upon rights and entitlement and which incorporates parental perspectives, experience and skills as complementary to professionals' and practitioners' own expertise. In this model, parents become active contributors rather than passive recipients of services.

Eliciting parents' views and determining their needs for services: examples from research and practice

Approaches to consulting parents within education, social services, health, voluntary/national organisations can and do vary: they include large- and small-scale distance surveys via questionnaire; one-to-one interviews; focus groups. Sometimes these methods set out to explore family situations and thereby to determine levels of perceived need.

Examples include large-scale surveys of parents of children with disabilities and special needs (Beresford 1994, SCOPE 1994, MENCAP 1997, Kagan *et al.* 1998). The data obtained can be used to try to effect a match between need and provision; however there is little published information as to the direct use that service managers, agency personnel do make from such rich and accessible information on what parents themselves feel their needs are.

Examples of a smaller-scale approach, involving individual interviews with parents and carers of young children with special needs and those with mental health problems is the research undertaken by the Children's Society (Widdows 1997) and that of the Mental Health Foundation (1997). Whether large or smaller-scale, such investigations could be regarded as **prospective** in anticipating and auditing the nature and extent of expressed parental needs for services.

Some local social services departments were very 'parent-friendly' in preparing their Childrens' Services Plans (CSP) and fully consulted local parents/carers, or representative groups of local parents, and others barely paid lip service to this aspect of the consultation process. In their review of CSPs Hearn and Sinclair (1998) see a definite place for the inclusion of families, *including children and young people*, in needs analyses and this view is supported by Ball (1998a) who has a generally positive view about trends: 'The apparatus provided by the CSP to co-ordinate and develop family-centred approaches is now familiar and there is a growing understanding about using it. At field level there are many examples of good practice, across agencies and in listening to families' (p.61).

In contra-distinction to 'needs' audit being prospective and pro-active, parents' views have been sought **retrospectively** as part of evaluation of provision. Examples include the evaluation of LEA special needs Parent Partnership Schemes, undertaken by Wolfendale and Cook (1997) for the Department for Education and Employment (DfEE). We held focus groups of between 6 and 12 parents/carers of children with special educational needs in 25 LEAs and asked their views about the service they had been receiving from their local parent partnership scheme and also what progress they felt had been made locally towards partnership with parents. Their opinions formed a crucial part of the research; in fact they were the barometer by which progress could be judged.

Parents' and carers' views can be sought **concurrently** – that is, during a programme, a piece of intervention, a provision. This model is now built into the OFSTED school inspection process, via the pre-inspection parental questionnaire and the meeting between inspectors and parents. The data from such exercises helps to inform the inspection process and must be included in the inspection report.

Home-school Agreements (HSA), a provision of the 1998 Education (School Standards and Framework) Act, can also be a vehicle for the expression of parental views. The introduction of HSA (DfEE 1998) from 1 September 1999 marks a significant shift in educational democracy. A HSA is a statement explaining the school's aims and values; the school's responsibilities towards its pupils; the responsibilities of the parents; what the school expects of its pupils. However, as part of the process of developing a HSA, it is encumbent upon schools and their governing bodies to review their existing home-school policy and to consult with their constituencies of parents about determining the form and scope of the proposed HSA, and equally, about its subsequent revision.

Another example of concurrent as well as retrospective parental input comes from the parent education and support programme run in the London Borough of Newham for the past three years. Bopinder Samra was the programme coordinator and I was the evaluator (see Chapter 8). We devised weekly short evaluation sheets for parent-participants to complete and held post-programme focus groups of the participating parents. From analysis of these responses from dozens of such courses over three years, we grouped parental responses into these eight themes:

- general value for parents in their role as parents;
- value in their role as behaviour manager;
- specific skill gains;
- learning practical strategies;
- confirmation that they are not alone, in having parental anxieties and lack of confidence;
- having greater understanding of the parental role;
- general gains in confidence in being a parent;
- having realistic expectations.

(Wolfendale 1997b)

The ongoing evaluation provided valuable monitoring data, which complemented outcome data, i.e. end of programme feedback. In fact, process data could well be less blunt and more situation-sensitive than endpoint data.

An example of pervasive parental consultation, prospective, concurrent, retrospective, is that of the special educational needs early years intervention programme, Portage, within which parents are partners in designing and delivering (as 'teachers' to their young children in learning and skill acquisition) and reviewing. It is an inherent part of the Portage model (White 1997) that parents are represented on multi-disciplinary Portage management teams.

Messages from parents/carers concerning needs for and from services

There is a marked similarity in theme and message coming through from parents from surveys, questionnaire returns and interviews over many years as to what they need on behalf of their children, their families, themselves. What was identified in the Warnock Report (Warnock 1978) on special education has been a subsequent recurring theme, namely that parents want and need easy availability of information about service provision and straight-forward access to it.

This is a brief summary of what data from the various sources cited in this chapter tells us about parents' needs for services:

> parents want accessible information about accessible services and the availability of support. Depending upon the focus, parents also need periodic respite from or support with stressful responsibilities. They do need to feel that professionals can engage, temporarily but fully, with their (parental) problems. They do want to be treated with respect on a basis of equality, and on the premise that they too have much to contribute to the development and education of their children. They do wish to part a play in decision-making over provision.

Does inter-agency cooperative practice incorporate parental perspectives?

The conspicuous lack of effective inter-agency liaison has been well chronicled over many years and a number of models and blueprints have been outlined to eradicate endemic structural, experiential and attitudinal factors that have militated against greater cooperation (see Jones and Bilton 1994). Some of the historical problems are summarised thus, in Ball (1998a): 'We know...about the lack of collaborative, inter-agency assessments of children; the lack of clear information about eligibility for services; and the lack of inter-agency protocols for dealing with shared and overlapping responsibilities' (from Foreword, unpaged).

Such integral barriers to inter-agency liaison have not been conducive to the incorporation of parental views into decision-making, and in fact, despite between-agency communication difficulties, 'it remains true that the major agencies, whether they work separately or collaboratively, tend to find the voice of the professional the easiest both to listen to and to articulate' (Dyson *et al.* 1998, p.12). These authors go on to state, and this is key to the thesis advanced in this chapter, 'The effectiveness of inter-agency cooperation, therefore, has to be judged against not only the extent to which it meets professional concerns, but also the extent to which the voice of the child and parent is heard in decisions about how, where and to whom services will be provided' (p. 12).

Recommendations along these lines could easily remain at the level of rhetoric and exhortation. However, Ball (1998a) provides a number of encouraging examples wherein cooperative endeavours between agencies, on behalf of disabled children, have developed 'family friendly' approaches that incorporate parental (and children's) views. 'Consultation is not an easy process, but research evidence suggests that it is an essential one'.

Hallmarks of an inclusive approach to planning and delivering services

We now have a sufficient number of indicators from many sources as to what could constitute the building blocks of child- and family-focused services, including parenting education and support. There are a sufficient number of models and methodologies for us to proceed with providing intervention and services that are preventative as well as problem-focused.

There are several sources to support the contention that a 'family friendly', democratic-egalitarian inclusive approach involving parents as partners in service design and delivery is the way forward. These include:

- Sinclair, Hearn and Pugh (1997): their attributes of effective services are their 'seven As' (p.45) *available, acceptable, affordable, accessible, accountable, appropriate, across-agency.*

- Carpenter (1997): from an international comparison of three early years intervention programmes, several key themes emerged, paramount amongst which was

  the unifying factor...was that, there was a recognition of the parent as an implicit and fundamental member of that team... parents were integral to the whole operation. Not only were they the recipients of services but also were seen as service deliverers themselves. There was a recognition of their unique and invaluable contribution' (p.24).

- Talay-Ongan (1998): propounds a number of basic tenets in working with families, within a broad ecological framework; tenets which include respecting, valuing and embracing families' contexts and which emphasise the reciprocal nature of the professional-parental relationship in these words:

  the primary professional role is to support the family in making decisions and stating individual preferences regarding services for their children (p.297).

She regards heeding parental views as a central aspect of services planning.

Towards a partnership model

(a) A rationale for a partnership model

This part of the chapter proposes a partnership model that includes the expression of parental needs for services such as a parenting programme as well as the parents' participation in design and delivery.

The rationale rests on a number of imperatives, moral, educational and economic. The core elements within each are set out below:

Moral Imperatives
- Parents have *rights* and *entitlement* to be thus involved.
- Parents are equal partners; their involvement is predicated upon principles of *equity* and *reciprocity.*
- The *raison d'être* of services is to *make a positive difference* to the quality of children's and families' lives.

Educational Imperatives
- Parents are the first educators of their children.
- Parents have the prime responsibility for the care and rearing of their children.
- By virtue of their role as first educator, parents are partners in learning with their children's teachers.
- Parents provide growth and learning opportunities at home, within a loving and caring context (see Chapter 7).

Economic Imperatives
The basic premise here is that direct participation of parents at all stages constitutes:
- Value for money, cost effectiveness, 'best-buys' of services/ intervention/programmes by involving the 'clients' and effecting a match between identified need and service provision.
- This represents an efficient use of resources.
- There is concomitant financial accountability, and parent-recipients themselves understand and are party to financial decision-making.

Essentially, services for children, parents/carers and families are about supporting the parental role and parenting responsibilities.

(b) Introducing a model for partnership and inclusivity

A summary of approaches shows us that prevalent practice includes *prospective, concurrent* and *retrospective* methods of eliciting parental views and their estimates of their need for services and provision. Drawing upon this conceptual framework a model is presented below which outlines parental involvement on the basis of equity at each stage from (1) needs analysis, service and programme design, to (2) service and programme delivery, to (3) post-service and programme review and evaluation. The model is intentionally eclectic, that is, it has applicability to a range of family-focused intervention and is therefore considered particularly appropriate for parenting education and support programmes, which are usually discrete, time-limited, funding-dependent, with identifiable goals and anticipated outcomes.

(c) *Components of the Model*
Prospective (needs analysis, service and programme design)

- local audit of existing services (such as required by the 1989 Children Act, and by Early Years partnerships)
- local surveys of target 'consumers' to ascertain levels and types of need (as well as drawing upon existing evidence bases of need) (and see Ball 1997)
- inclusion of parents/parent representatives into the planning via local planning fora/programme steering/planning group/ research committee; a necessary concomitant here would be provision of training and support for parents to develop the confidence to participate, become empowered, even politicised for such action (see also Chapter 6 of this volume)
- consultation with parents over the programme content and style of delivery
- agree ethical 'ground rules' or Code of Conduct governing all participants (Wolfendale 1999).

Concurrent (service and programme delivery)

- parental input/representation on steering/monitoring group
- sampling 'users' views for the duration on a regular or periodic basis (see Newham example earlier in the chapter and Wolfendale 1997b)
- adherence to the Code of Conduct.

Retrospective (post-service/programme review and evaluation)
- parental input/representation on steering/review group
- end of programme survey via questionnaire, interview, focus groups
- review and evaluation of programme and conduct by all partici-pants (see Van der Eyken *et al.* 1997 for ideas on self-evaluation, Grimshaw and McGuire 1998, and Chapter 11 in this book).

Dissemination of outcomes to a wider constitutency of parents and local community would form an important component of review as part of accountability and quality assurance.

I do not underestimate the challenge of moving towards an egalitarian, reciprocal way of working. Parents may be unused to being consulted and professionals may be constrained by tradition and professional conventions and assumptions as Dale (1996) expresses in these words: 'assumptions (by professionals) of what the parent wants and needs get in the way of finding out what the parent *really* wants and needs' (p.157). She suggests how to develop an individual family services plan using a Negotiating Model (p.160). This is but one approach but serves well to illustrate the necessary building in of a sufficient number of steps, at each of which the 'negotiating parties' can pause, take stock before proceeding towards the mutually agreed goals. To be realistic, perhaps conflict resolution strategies have to be an inbuilt part of any arrangement whereby different vested interests could potentially lead to dissonance.

But it is time to shake off and reverse the traditional 'dominant discourse' promoted and maintained by practitioners (Moss and Petrie 1997) and reform our view of the parent-professional relationship. The Early Childhood Unit at the National Children's Bureau has produced a set of performance indicators for services planners (National Children's Bureau 1998, p.21) which shows how, irrespective of what the service or provision is – and it could include parenting education and support programmes – inclusion of parents and carers into the planning and delivery form integral performance indicators.

Taking collective responsibility for an inclusive approach

It is anticipated that, with flagship national fora such as the Parenting Forum and the National Family and Parenting Institute proposed in the Home Office Consultation Document *Supporting Families* (Home Office 1998), the area of parenting education and support will continue to grow significantly. As other authors within this book affirm (for example, see Chapter 10 by Peter Jones) the area is transdisciplinary, and no agency or discipline has a particular monopoly on hosting programmes, courses, training. Dwivedi (1998) in his editor's introduction lists many professionals from disciplines within education, health, social services, voluntary agencies who can have a legitimate brief for 'enhancing parenting skills' (p.4) and see Ball (1998b) and Smith (1996),

Dwivedi's book also emphasises how there is an onus on professional deliverers of parenting programmes to acknowledge and incorporate cultural, religious, social and familial diversity within their programmes (and see Barnardo's Report 1997). At the time of the inception of the Parenting Forum in 1995, this author contributed a paper to one of the founding conferences at the National Children's Bureau which aimed to promote a framework for appraising the extent to which programme aims are met by the delivery of a parenting education programme. A set of twelve aims,

.sed upon a number of key underpinning values were formulated which were these:

- incorporates multi-cultural family factors;
- actively challenges role, gender and racist stereotyping;
- tackles socio-economic differences and their influence upon parenting;
- values diversity of family composition;
- handles and discusses disparate child rearing attitudes and practices;
- explicitly appeals to *all* parents;
- operates a 'wealth' model of family heritage yet identifies family needs;
- promotes empowerment of parents;
- emphasizes parents' existing skills;
- fosters new skills for parents;
- explores parental responsibility;
- tackles children's and parents' rights.

This is a challenging set of aims and their exploration within parenting programmes would not necessarily be comfortable for parent-participants nor professional organisers.

Returning full-circle to the premise advanced at the beginning of the chapter, parenting education and support programmes stand a better chance of successful realisation if parents and carers are equal partners and therefore key determinants at all stages. The central message is that successful childrearing is a collective familial and societal responsibility, and parents and carers themselves are equal stakeholders.

References

Ball, M. (1997) *Consulting with Parents, guidelines for good practice.* The National Early Years Network, 77 Holloway Road, London N7 8JZ.

Ball, M. (1998a) *Disabled Children: directions for their future care.* Social Services Inspectorate/Department of Health, copies from Department of Health, PO Box 410, Wetherby LS23 7LN.

Ball, M. (1998b) *School Inclusion – the school, the family and the community.* Joseph Rowntree Foundation, The Homestead, 40 Water End, York YO30 6WP.

Barnardo's (1997) *Today and Tomorrow, investing in our children.* Barnardos, Tanners Lane, Barkingside, Ilford, Essex IG6 1QG.

Beresford, B. (1994) *Expert Opinions, a national survey of parents caring for a severely disabled child.* Joseph Rowntree Foundation/The Policy Press, University of Bristol, Rodney Lodge, Grange Road, Bristol BS8 4EA.

Carpenter, B. (ed.) (1997) *Families in Context, emerging trends in family support and early intervention.* London: David Fulton Publishers.

Dale, N. (1996) *Working with Families of Children with Special Needs.* London: Routledge.

DfEE (1998) *Home School Agreements, guidance for schools* (ref. PPY984), DfEE Publications, PO Box 5050, Sudbury, Suffolk CO10 6ZQ.

Dwivedi, K. (ed.) (1997) *Enhancing Parenting Skills, a guide for professionals working with parents.* Chichester, John Wiley and Sons.

Dyson, A., Lin, M., Millward, A. (1998) *Effective Communication between Schools, LEAs and Health and Social Services in the Field of SEN,* DfEE Research Report, RR60, DfEE Publications, PO Box 5050, Sudbury, Suffolk CO10 6ZQ

Grimshaw, R. and McGuire, C. (1998) *Evaluating Parenting Programmes, a study of stakeholders' views,* London: National Children's Bureau and Joseph Rowntree Foundation.

Hearn, B. and Sinclair, R. (1998) *Children's Services Plans, analysing need: reallocating resources, a report to the Department of Health.* London, National Children's Bureau.

Home Office (1998) *Supporting Families,* a Consultation Document. London: Stationery Office Group Ltd., October.

Jones, A. and Bilton, J. (1994) *The Future Shape of Children's Services.* London: National Children's Bureau.

Kagan, C., Lewis, S., Heaton, P. (1998) *Combining Work and Care: working parents of disabled children.* Joseph Rowntree Foundation, The Homestead, 40 Water End, York YO3 6LP.

MENCAP (1997) *Left in the Dark, a MENCAP report on the challenges facing the UK's 400,000 families of children with learning disabilities,* MENCAP, 123 Golden Lane. London: EC1Y 0RT.

Mental Health Foundation (1997) *Unconditional Love? the views and experiences of parents living with children with mental health problems,* Mental Health Foundation, 37 Mortimer Street, London W1N 8JU.

Moss, P. and Petrie, P. (1997) *Children's Services, time for a new approach, a discussion paper,* Thomas Coram Research Unit, London University Institute of Education.

National Children's Bureau/Early Childhood Unit (1998) *Planning, Partnership and Equality for Young Children, a practical guide.* London: National Children's Bureau.

SCOPE (1994) *Right from the Start, Looking at Diagnosis and Disclosure – parents describe how they found out about their child's disability,* SCOPE, 12 Park Crescent, London W1N 4EQ.

Sinclair, R., Hearn, B., Pugh, G. (1997) *Preventive Work with Families, the role of mainstream services.* London: National Children's Bureau.

Smith, C. (1996) *Developing Parenting Programmes.* London, National Children's Bureau.

Talay-Ongan, A. (1998) *Typical and Atypical Development in Early Childhood.* Leicester: British Psychological Society Books.

Van der Eyken, W., Williams, S., Vallender, I. (1997) *Finding out, an informal guide to self-evaluation of family centres,* National Council for Voluntry Child Care Organisations, Unit, 4, Pride Court, 80–82 White Lion Street, London N1 9PF.

Warnock, M. (Chair) (1978) *Special Educational Needs.* The Warnock Report. London: HMSO (now Stationery Office Group Ltd).

White, M. (1997) 'A review of the influence and effects of Portage', Chapter Two in Wolfendale, S. (ed.) *Working with Parents of SEN Children after the Code of Practice*, London: David Fulton Publishers.

Widdows, J. (1997) *A Special Need for Inclusion, children with disabilities, their families and everyday life*, The Children's Society, Edward Rudolf House, 4 Margery Street, London WC1X 0JL.

Wolfendale, S. (ed.) (1997a) *Working with Parents of SEN Children after the Code of Practice*. London: David Fulton Publishers.

Wolfendale, S. (1997b) *City Challenge: action for achievement, fourth evaluation report, 1996–1997*. Psychology Department, University of East London.

Wolfendale, S. (1999) 'Parents as partners in research and evaluation: methodological and ethical issues and solutions', *British Journal of Special Education*.

Wolfendale, S. and Cook, G. (1997) *Evaluation of SEN Parent Partnership Schemes*, DfEE Research Report No. 34, DfEE Publications, PO Box 5050, Sudbury, Suffolk CO10 6ZQ.

SECTION TWO:

Themes of parental identity and contexts for parenting

Chapter 5

Being a parent: influences and effects upon parenting from the media

Lucy McCarraher

Over the last three decades, media studies and research have attempted to ascertain the effects of the media on the behaviour and attitudes of children and to determine the longer-term results of their exposure to certain types of television and video. A conflict of methodologies has arisen between researchers who favour the 'Media Effects' approach and those who have developed 'Media Reception' studies. The latter takes greater account of interactions outside the media viewed and subsequent behaviour to include individual predisposition, social conditions, peer groups, changing technology and the role of the media itself. No studies to date, though, have focused on the role of parents in their children's response to the media, nor examined parents' own relationship to the media and the effect this may have on their children. In a climate where social and governmental pressure is growing for mothers and fathers to be more professional in their role as parents, the media as a source of information, positive and/or negative, has been largely ignored.

Family Viewing, a report on parents, children and the media (McCarraher 1998) is the first study into this area and examines parents' responses to media influences on themselves and their children. The results of the research suggest a strongly interactive relationship between parents, children and the media, with each element constantly reacting with the other two in the fertile cultures of individual home environments.

This chapter outlines the main findings about how parents use the media as a support and source of information and in what areas they find it fails them. Whilst they draw on obvious sources for information such as factual programmes, parents also consciously absorb more covert messages from drama and comedy. They actively use the media and its subject matter as a means of relating to their children and assess its impact daily on their sons and daughters. Parents also access the relaxation and stress relief it offers as a conscious aid to their work as mothers and fathers. They recognise the power of the media to represent and to support them, but are not satisfied with the media's recognition of them as parents and demand more in both quantity and quality of material aimed at them.

Current media culture

If it is true that 'People depend in large measure on the cultural industries for the images, symbols and vocabulary with which they interpret and respond to their social environment' (Golding and Murdock 1996), then parents as a group have less representation in the British media than cooks, gardeners, holiday-makers or DIY and car enthusiasts. All of these latter, and other niche market audiences, have several (some would say an excess of) programmes, series, dedicated magazines, columns and sections in newspapers and magazines which cater to their specific interests, providing information and illustration as well as celebrity and 'real people' role models. Depiction and elucidation of these activities by the media validates those who participate in them and provide them with a positive social identity.

Parents, by contrast, have almost no programming dedicated to their needs and are therefore not reflected by the broadcast media as a group of people united and affirmed by the activity they are engaged in. This lack of information about and coverage of their work and interests, particularly in comparison to that of other domestic and leisure activities, actively lowers their perceived social worth. Added to this, the representation of parents in television drama, comedy and advertising is often through stereotyped, opaque and patronising images and models.

A number of magazines aimed at parents-to-be and parents of younger children are published and 'sections' of newspapers and magazines aimed at women, particularly, are inclined to include parenting subjects in a more comprehensive and integrated way. Magazines whose market is clearly women with children do address family and parenting issues as one of many important roles their readers play out in their lives. Men's magazines, however, very rarely address their readers as fathers or parents, although the image of 'the caring father' has recently been much exploited by advertisers of products such as cars, financial services and men's clothing.

The Parenting Education and Support Forum research project into parents, children and the media sought to understand more about the media as a context in which contemporary mothers and fathers derive their identity as parents and the role the media plays in supporting and informing parents at the end of the twentieth century. Working with project partners, NSPCC, Glasgow Media Group and *Family Circle* magazine, the project followed efforts by the Forum's Parenting and Media Working Group to encourage broadcasters to develop and schedule ongoing series aimed at the needs of parents. These efforts were met almost uniformly with expressions of interest and agreement on the importance of the subject, but no resulting programming. The ground-breaking results of the research are being used as a marketing tool with broadcasters and other media as well as pointing the way towards the need for further research.

Current parenting culture

> In order to maintain the viability of their position in society, [media professionals] must be closely attuned to the spirit of the times, reflecting the cultural ethos of society and, indeed, at times serving as its leading edge. (Gurevitch and Blumler 1993)

The research with parents, through a survey carried in *Family Circle* magazine May 1998 and focus groups, as well as personal and professional experience, indicated that the 'spirit of the times' is placing increasing value on and interest in the function of parents and families in generating a positive and well-balanced society. The current Labour government has indicated a commitment to supporting families and parents, to which large sections of the media (from tabloid newspaper to 'serious' reportage) have responded with accusations of a 'nanny' state attempting to enforce education in an area which they believe is and should be 'instinctive' and 'natural'. The same commentators are equally likely to blame inadequate parents for youth crime, unmotivated young people, a young 'underclass' and other social ills. In this area, few elements of the media are reflecting the cultural ethos of society, let alone serving as its leading edge.

One indication of a culture attaining maturity is a desire to see itself accurately reflected in its own arts and media. 'Young' nations such as Canada, Australia and some African countries, which had previously been dominated by older or more powerful cultures, have at strategic times implemented quotas of indigenous television programming, theatre production and other art forms. It has been an important phase in the development of their cultural identity to see themselves (as opposed to English or American characters, accents, settings and situations) represented as the social norm on their screens and stages. The sub-culture of parenting and family awareness appears to have entered such a phase; parents avidly watch and comment on the family relationships and dramas within soaps and dramas, the activities of celebrity parents and those of 'real' people appearing on confessional and discussion programmes. The media establishment, however, is presently lagging behind the public perception and desire for recognition of parenting as a central issue in people's lives and has failed to capitalise on this by headlining and developing programming under this banner.

Broadcast media

In the survey to which 330 parents responded, participants were asked which television or radio programmes they found helpful to them as parents. Three quarters of respondents claimed they were helped by factual programming on children and parenting and just over half found news and children's programming of assistance. A little under half had been helped by consumer programmes. Perhaps more surprisingly, nearly a third cited drama and films and one fifth soap operas as programmes which were helpful to them as parents.

Comments written on questionnaires and focus group discussion suggested that there were three main ways in which these categories of programme were used by parents.

The first and largest was in adding to parents' knowledge about parenting and their children. As well as the above categories, parents nominated discussion programming and even cartoons like *Stressed Eric* and *King of the Hill* – 'anything which shows families trying to learn' – as useful in this way. All the focus groups mentioned having their awareness of certain issues raised by soap opera coverage of, for instance, HIV and the termination of a spina bifida baby on *EastEnders* and a baby's death from meningitis on *Coronation Street*. Radio programmes such as phone-in discussions on Talk Radio, items on *Woman's Hour* and *You and Yours* and programmes that featured 'real people' like *Home Truths* on Radio 4 were mentioned as providing useful information and support.

Some criticism was voiced in focus groups of documentary programmes such as *Panorama* and *World in Action* for only covering parenting and family issues from an extreme and sensational point of view.

The second way in which television programmes helped parents was in entertaining and informing their children, as well as raising subjects for discussion between parents and children. Focus group participants nominated many television series and programmes which they felt had a positive effect on their children.

For younger children, the most popular programme was *Teletubbies*. Parents were scornful of criticisms which suggested the content was not educational enough for very young children and agreed that its open-ended and comparatively slow-moving format allowed young children to develop their own imaginations. Other series which were felt to have a positive influence on younger children included *Thomas the Tank Engine, Postman Pat, Fireman Sam, Barney* and Disney films.

For older children, positive influences were agreed by all focus groups to include traditional children's series, but the most regularly nominated were all nature and wildlife programmes and, specifically, *Blue Peter*, *Animal Hospital* and *Children's Hospital*. Parents found these programmes to be informative and to provide good modelling (such as caring for other people, animals or the environment), but they also valued them because they raise areas of discussion between parents and children.

Most focus group participants said their children of all ages also watched 'adult' television such as soaps, discussion programmes, such as *Kilroy* and *Vanessa* and some of the American series such as *Oprah Winfrey*, *Jerry Springer* and *Montel*. Younger children tended to watch these when their parents did and some worried that issues were covered in these programmes which were not suitable for younger children.

Parents of older children (over the age of eight), though, felt it was helpful to them that these sorts of issues were raised by such series and that they gave them a chance to discuss subjects like sex, homosexuality, AIDS and drugs which might not have been talked about spontaneously. Despite recent criticisms of questionable practice of 'discussion' or 'confessional' programmes such as *Vanessa* and *Jerry Springer* (Independent Television Commission 1998), the parents who responded to the survey and took part in focus groups, did not express negative views about them.

The third way in which parents felt helped by television programmes, was simply through the personal relaxation offered by watching comedy, drama, soaps or sport.

Thirty-eight per cent of the 330 parents surveyed said that something they had watched on television or heard on the radio had influenced their behaviour or attitude towards their children. A high number of survey respondents said that television or radio programmes had given them greater understanding of their children, their views and attitudes, and made them more 'open-minded'. Programmes had also given them fresh ideas for dealing with problems, for entertaining and stimulating their children. Many parents reported feeling supported and reinforced in their belief that they were doing a 'good enough' job as parents; similar numbers were relieved to find other parents in comparable predicaments or using strategies akin to their own. Several said they had seen or heard programmes that encouraged them to listen and communicate better with their children, rethink, for example, their attitude to smacking and give more praise for good behaviour.

A few parents said that radio and television programmes had made them more aware of dangers outside the home, such as bullying, drugs and paedophiles, and this had in some cases made them more protective of their children. This was not presented as a positive response and could be seen as related to the 'sensationalist' coverage remarked on earlier. The general consensus, though, was that parents took positive messages from radio and television and valued their children more as a result.

Eighty-two per cent of survey respondents said they would like to see more programmes on television to help and advise parents. 'The media has a big role to play in educating people, letting people know that they are not the only ones in any situation.' This quote sums up the attitude of focus groups and many comments written on questionnaires. In fact there was a certain incredulity that so many informational programmes were devoted to topics like gardening, pets, cars, sex, cooking and DIY, but that broadcasters were not prepared to offer anything similar to parents. In the words of another focus group participant, 'when you put it in the context of pet shows and garden shows, it's pretty obvious that TV has a duty to provide parenting and family information'.

The only stipulations were that any programmes on parenting should not be dictatorial or guilt-inducing, nor aimed at 'bad' parents.

Contrary to current broadcast scheduling, the majority of parents would prefer to watch television programming on family issues in the evening, rather than during the day. A late evening timeslot was by far the most popular, with over 60 per cent of survey respondents preferring to watch when children were in bed, though over 40 per cent would watch in the early evening. Under one quarter wanted programming in the morning and under one fifth in the afternoon. The fact is, most parents are simply not available to watch television during the day: in 1994, 59 per cent of mothers and 85 per cent of fathers in the UK were in employment (Brannen *et al.* 1994) and the figure for mothers is rising. Of the focus group participants who were not in paid work and were caring for children full time, most still preferred to watch programmes on parenting or children's issues in the evening. Daytime television programmes, they felt, were not taken seriously by either broadcasters or viewers. A mother of an eight month old baby said, 'Young mums like me might watch a programme at lunchtime while we're feeding the baby, but the evening's better for more serious, reflective programmes.'

Fathers wanted to watch programmes on parenting and mothers were particularly keen for such programmes to be on when their partners were around to watch. Both felt it was important that they were not just aimed at mothers, but at fathers too.

A number of focus group participants and survey respondents said they were more likely to listen to radio programmes rather than watch television during the day as they could do so while continuing with other activities. They also felt that daytime radio took a more in-depth and serious perspective than daytime television programming. Several parents suggested radio programmes on parenting and family issues could usefully be broadcast to fit in with caring responsibilities, such as during the times of school runs.

The questionnaire asked respondents which areas they would most want to see covered by television programmes on parenting or family issues. Children's behaviour was by far the favourite subject with 72 per cent wanting to access programming covering this; it was closely followed by education issues, discipline, children's psychological development and health issues. Over half wanted to see relationships covered in parenting programming and almost half wanted information in programming about balancing work and family.

There was much discussion in focus groups on further subject matter participants would like to see covered in a regular parenting series and many respondents wrote detailed suggestions on questionnaires. The most popular unprompted proposals included consumer advice about all aspects of children and families from car seats and baby walkers, to educational toys, holidays, school uniform and playschemes; seasonal reminders about looming educational milestones and health issues; dealing with parents' own stress, anger and relaxation; issues of single mothers and fathers and non-stereotyped gender roles; techniques to improve listening and communication with children; the importance of play and keeping families fun; and coping with siblings.

Above all, parents repeated that they wanted to see how other people, 'real people', coped with the same problems as them, felt the same emotions and found individual solutions to the wide-ranging scenarios of family life. They did not want to hear single experts pontificating on a particular viewpoint, although they would be interested in hearing a range of experts debate an issue. Nor did they want to be informed only about issues which related to their own situation or children's ages. The survey and focus groups both showed parents hungry for knowledge across the board about families like and unlike their own, to inform and support them and their peer group in the widest possible sense. There was evidence of a strong feeling of solidarity between parents and a desire to be taken seriously and addressed intelligently in this role by the media.

All the focus groups, when asked about their ideal programming on parenting issues, suggested a weekly, ongoing, evening series, with wide-ranging subject matter in a magazine format along the lines of a gardening or DIY series. Presenters should be 'people who are quite warm, quite caring' and certainly parents themselves. Focus group participants thought it was essential that there should be a male and female presenter of such a series, as 'men have a problem taking advice from women' and 'it would be good for dads to have a man talking about what it's like to care for kids'.

Indeed, there was a strong feeling from both the survey and focus groups that parents anticipated a powerful influence from strong parenting television programming in bolstering their self-confidence, improving their own and public perception of parents, and in generating acceptability for social change and challenging accepted norms.

Television programming on parenting issues has perhaps been subject to similar assumptions of cultural competence as soap operas up until the early 1980s. Until that point it was assumed that this was a 'woman's' genre and therefore an inferior media form which anyone could understand, but in which only a low intelligence audience would be interested. Hence many soaps were scheduled during the day and aimed at a predominantly female audience. It later became clear with more in-depth research that soap viewers would accept such patronising and chauvinistic assumptions on the part of broadcasters 'in order to engage with the themes of personal, domestic life and intimate, often family relationships' (Branston and Stafford 1996).

As well as having an interest in the domestic and personal experiences that form the subject matter of soaps, female viewers also understood the conventions of the genre and were able to read, for instance, looks between characters, silences and small-scale gestures in which much of the meaning resides. 'The group most likely to have such knowledge was women, with their informal training as mothers or...carers' (Branston and Stafford 1996). Once they accepted a more sophisticated level of audience involvement, broadcasters and producers were proactive in incorporating more plots and themes with 'male' interest, which resulted in the broader-based, prime time successes such as *EastEnders* and *Brookside*. It could, indeed, be argued that attracting a male audience to soaps has been a significant element in fostering men's increasing involvement in domestic and caring life. As our focus group participants pointed out, seeing it on television can validate social change in real life.

The results of the research, revealing parents' appetite for ongoing, evening programming aimed at fathers and mothers, strongly suggest that programmes on parenting issues could be travelling a similar route to that of the soap opera and therefore poised to become a popular, prime time genre. Another indicator of their high ratings potential lies in the frequency with which 'discussion' programmes were mentioned in our survey as a source of information, 'real people's' experience and starting points for family debate. While such series as *Vanessa* and *Jerry Springer* are typically decried for their lack of professional input, voyeuristic approach and exploitation of subjects, it seems likely that parents (among others) watch them as the only available currency in relationship, social and parent/child issues that they seek. Higher quality programmes more specifically suited to their needs will surely be met with an enthusiastic response.

Print media

Survey respondents, totalling 330, were asked whether they regularly bought a parenting/family magazine and 20 per cent said they did. The survey was carried in *Family Circle* magazine, so it was, not surprisingly, the most popularly nominated title. It was followed by *Practical Parenting*, then the BBC's *Family Life*. Other magazines mentioned by several respondents were *Parentwise*, *Mother and Baby*, *Parents*, *Right Start* and *Fun For Kids*. Single nominations went to *Parenting*, *Child* (American), *Natural Parent*, *Living*, *Nursery World*, *Family Health*, *Christian Woman*, *Prima*, *Best*, *Bella*, *Our Baby* and *Junior*.

This list reveals that there are a considerable number of magazine titles aimed at parents of young children and women's magazines covering parenting and family issues. Most parents said they read, or had read, magazines when they were pregnant and their children were young, but stopped doing so as they got older. This was in large part because of a lack of magazines on parenting of children over the age of eight or nine, which participants deplored.

Thirty-five per cent of parents or carers said something they had read in a magazine had influenced their behaviour or attitude towards their children. Examples of this included information on children's behaviour, health issues and healthy eating, understanding of and communicating with small children, sleeping and eating problems, dealing with tantrums and coping strategies. Again, parents said magazine articles helped them to rethink and re-evaluate their parenting and that on the whole they were given confidence by what they read. A small minority said they were made to feel guilty by magazines on parenting. As with television, many said they enjoyed and benefited from 'real life' case histories.

Unlike their broad-based attitude to information from television, parents seemed to want magazine articles to be more specific to their own situation and looked for different types of material, more 'hard' information like consumer material and dietary facts, which they often kept for reference. This slightly different emphasis between broadcast and publications was borne out in the responses to the question about which areas parents would like to see covered in magazines on family issues. Again, the subject of children's behaviour took top priority for parents, but was followed by health, then education, children's psychological development, discipline, relationships and balancing work and family.

Other areas that respondents nominated as wanting to see covered included parenting behaviour, entertaining children, positive parenting, building self-esteem, support for non-working mothers, budgeting, spiritual development and information on older children.

A number of focus group participants said that they regularly read parenting and family articles in more general magazines and 74 per cent of survey respondents said they read advice on parenting or family issues in the newspapers. Several focus group participants felt that although there was sometimes valuable material to be found in newspapers there was not enough coverage of parenting or family issues in general. Often issues were treated as news stories and headlined, but then not followed up in a way useful to parents, leaving them unsure of the facts and their options for response.

One focus group mother suggested a reason for lack of coverage on parenting and family issues in newspapers: 'probably because it's mostly put together by men'.

Role models

The media's influence is subtle as well as overt in all fields, including parenting. Consciously or unconsciously, public figures and fictional characters are portrayed by the media in a range of roles, including that of parent. Role models play a vital part in shaping our perception of what constitutes 'good' or 'bad' parenting. The research project tried to scratch the surface of this subliminal media influence by asking in the questionnaire which of the following 'media' figures respondents would rate as 'good' parents.

To their credit, a large minority of survey respondents declined to answer this question on the basis that judging others as parents was invidious or that they had no first hand information about these people as parents.

Of those who did respond to this question, 88 percent thought Cherie Blair, wife of Prime Minister Tony Blair, was a good parent and 68 per cent found Jack Straw, the present Home Secretary, to be a good parent (this was after he had dealt with his son's involvement with marijuana). There was a big drop then to the 50 per cent who rated Cathy Mitchell, a character from *EastEnders* as a good parent, 48 per cent who said the Duchess of York, 46 per cent who thought entrepreneur Bob Geldof and 45 per cent who considered the pop star Madonna good parents. Around one third felt that business-woman Nicola Horlick was a good parent (though many asked 'who?') and fewer still thought media personality Paula Yates one (this was before her suicide attempt). Phil Mitchell, husband of Cathy, from *EastEnders* came last with a six per cent vote.

It was notable that the most popularly perceived 'good' parent in the media was a full-time working mother and the second a (working) man, as was the most frequent unprompted nomination. They have in common that despite high profile positions, all three make it clear that their family life is a high priority and attempt to maintain both normality and privacy for their children.

We also asked for other nominations for 'good' media parents, and at the top of this list was music veteran Paul McCartney (his wife Linda McCartney was also mentioned. Questionnaires were likely to have been filled in around the time of her death). The second most nominated good media parent was actress Maureen Lipman, followed by Princess Diana and presenter John Peel. Others included television personalities Carole Vorderman, Anne Diamond, Jane Asher, Steve Chalk, Gary Rhodes, David Bellamy, Bill Cosby, Gloria Hunniford, Esther Rantsen and Pamela Armstrong; fictional characters Grant Mitchell (from *EastEnders*) and Shula Archer (from *The Archers*); MPs Clare Short and, Dafydd Wigley; royal parents Prince Charles and the Duke and Duchess of York; and commentators Barbara Toner, Frances Lawrence and Claire Rayner. Parents were not asked for explanations for their unprompted nominations.

Wish list

Finally, the 330 parents and carers were asked where they would ideally like to be able to find information or support. Television was the most favoured medium at 74 per cent, 67 per cent said they would like to find it in magazines and 54 per cent would like to find parenting information and support in newspapers. Under half would look for it on the radio, with just over one quarter seeking to find information on video and phonelines and the internet trailing at under one quarter.

The most popular alternative point of access nominated by respondents for parenting information and support were parenting classes. The next most nominated place where parents would like to find information were libraries, followed by GP surgeries, health centres, community centres and schools. This accords with other research which shows that doctors and teachers are the people to whom parents in need of help turn after family and friends (Ferri and Smith 1996). Other requests were for information and support through support groups, nurseries, workplaces, health visitors, Citizens' Advice Bureaux, adult education and Local Education Authorities.

Ways forward

Simon Frith points out in his article on 'Entertainment' (1996) that for the entertainment industry, 'public taste means "taste publics", patterns of leisure interest and activity that can be mapped onto other social characteristics – age and gender, class and ethnicity, sexuality and occupation, spending power... In this model what the public wants is effectively determined by who the public are.' The media in general and broadcasters in particular appear unable or unwilling to view parents or, more broadly, families, as a coherent market sector at whom they could profitably direct product. This seems short-sighted, especially in view of the extensive use advertisers and sponsors are making of images of family and parenting in selling and associating their products.

Advertisers and media organisations use class and occupation-based indicators to survey audiences which can be based on outdated models and thus provide inaccurate predictions of viewer/reader responses to innovative media concepts. Many, for instance, classify social class on the occupation of the 'head of the household', generally assumed to be a man and to some an offensive concept in itself. In an increasing number of households the main wage-earner is either a woman, or (because of shared caring responsibilities) the household income is made-up from part-time work by both partners. It is also common for surveys to view the family as a single unit and not break it down into generational or life-stage elements. Furthermore, old-style job categories often no longer coincide with the organisation or types of work now being done in the new flexible labour market. Indeed, the release of the new job-based social categories raises the question why caring and domestic commitments are not included as an indicator of status along with employment and income.

The responses of parents and carers of children to our survey give strong grounds for re-evaluating them as a major niche consumer market. If this is not revealed through current media reader and viewer profiles, then it is possible that new survey models should be developed which read more accurately contemporary social trends in families and caring commitments.

Whilst it can only be beneficial to both sides for the media to offer more information to families, there is also reason to provide more information to families about the media. Parents in the focus groups saw it as their duty to educate their children about advertising on television; this could be reinforced by stronger media education in schools from primary level upward. Even in the last five years the range of television available to children has increased exponentially and will continue to do so with the introduction of digital; the sophistication of advertising across the board has developed and the role and influence of all media become more diverse and complex. A better understanding of all these elements would equip both children and parents with a greater ability to gain maximum advantage from what is on offer and to challenge areas of manipulation. Providers of adult education or indeed parenting courses might usefully consider including or augmenting media literacy education components for parents.

It is to be hoped that government will back further research as part of its commitment to 'improve services and support for parents...encourage positive media involvement in raising the profile of family issues and...work with the media to increase and improve the coverage of issues of concern to parents' (Home Secretary, July 1998). Other bodies such as the British Board of Film Classification might also benefit from increased knowledge in how children and adults process the television and video they watch.

The findings of this initial piece of research might go some way towards convincing the broadcasting and print media that there is a sufficiently committed and sizeable audience and readership for material aimed at parents and families to bring them valuable sales, ratings, advertising and sponsorship. It would be unduly optimistic to believe that commercial organisations will be swayed by a social or moral imperative to provide parenting and family information for the good of their audiences (although the BBC is committed to servicing all interest groups in society and currently fails in this area). It is in theory possible for government to impose quotas of such programming on licensed broadcasters, as they do with religious and regional coverage, but parents and families are in the long run more likely to benefit from market-led product than imposed statutory or public service broadcasting or publishing campaigns. They are waiting to be recognised and reflected by the media to society at large as a coherent and cooperative group performing a vital, difficult, but stimulating and mainly enjoyable task – that of moulding the society and the parents of the future.

The *Family Viewing* research revealed that parents view the media as an influence for good, as well as bad in their children's lives. More research about the ways in which potential for the former can be realised and the latter reduced should be a priority for government and broadcasters alike. The means of acquiring this information is neither simple nor straightforward – 'it is clear that some laboratory experiments and other straightforward stimulus-response researches are seriously inadequate' (Miller and Philo 1998). The relationship between parents and the media, and between parents and their children are part of the complex weave through which we must seek to understand the influence of the media on children.

References

Brannen, J., Meszaros, G., Moss, P., Poland, G. (1994) *Employment and Family Life. A review of research in the UK* (1980–1994), 4. Sheffield: Employment Department.

Branston, G. and Stafford, R. (1996) *The Media Student's Book*, 322–3. London and New York: Routledge.

Independent Television Commission (1998) *Annual Report 1998*. Complaints upheld on *Jerry Springer*, broadcast 21 April 1998 and 24 April 1998 by UK Living and 15 May 1998 by LWT.

Family Circle magazine (May 1998) (IPC Magazines).

Ferri, E. and Smith, K. (1996) *Parenting in the 1990s*. London: Family Policy Studies Centre in association with the Joseph Rowntree Foundation.

Frith, S. (1996) 'Entertainment' in Curran, J. and Gurevitch, M. (eds) *Mass Media and Society*. London and New York: Michael Arnold.

Golding, P. and Murdock, G. (1996) 'Culture, communications and political economy', in Curran, J. and Gurevitch, M. (eds) *Mass Media and Society*. London and New York: Michael Arnold.

Gurevitch, M. and Blumler, J. G. (1993) 'Longtitudinal analysis of an election communication system: newsroom observation at the BBC 1966–1992', *Osterreichische Zeitschrift fur Politikwissenschaft*, **22** (4), 427–44.

Home Secretary's Speech (23 July 1998), 15. Launch of the Lords and Commons Family and Child Protection Group's Report *Family Matters*.

McCarraher, L. (1998) *Family Viewing, a report on parents, children and the media*. London: Parenting Education and Support Forum.

Miller, D. and Philo, G. (1998) 'Rethinking the effects debate: the media and violence' in Philo, G. (ed.) *Message Received, Glasgow Media Group Research 1993–1998*. London: Longman.

Chapter 6

Going critical: childhood, parenthood and the labour market

Peter Moss

Which way is the wind blowing?

> In recent years, there have been three major trends [in parental employment]: increasing integration of women with children, and particularly those with young children, into the labour market; increasing differentiation in mothers' employment opportunities and growing polarisation in household employment patterns; and an intensification of paid work amongst employed parents, contributing to a growing concentration of work – both paid and unpaid caring work – among women and men in the so-called 'prime working years' of 25 to 50 years. (Brannen and Moss 1998, p.230)

> The fact that more than half the people in Britain who are eligible to work are living either on poverty incomes or in conditions of permanent stress and insecurity [of employment] has had dreadful effects on the wider society. It has become harder and harder for men and women in these circumstances to hold their marriages together, let alone parent their children adequately, as the hours of work in which a decent wage can be earned grow longer and longer. (Hutton 1995, p.109)

> [Two decades into deregulation, liberalisation and bracing globalisation] money scours the world for the highest rate of return and, in doing so, it generates colossal instability. The role of governments is to maintain order in their territories (securing the operating base of multinational business) and package their populations into skilled, docile workforces with the correct attitudes in the hope that international finance may offer jobs through inward investment...the entire burden of risk, rather than being shared by people and business, is loaded onto the backs of people. (Atkinson and Elliott 1998)

Parenthood and employment in the 1990s

Employment has always been a preoccupation of parents, if for no other reason than its bearing on where the next meal might come from. But the preoccupation of parents – both fathers and mothers – with employment may well be increasing. Growing numbers of parents are in the labour force (up from 75 per cent in 1984 to 78 per cent in 1994 (Brannen *et al.* 1997)) as mothers join fathers in employment. This growth combined with falling employment amongst young people and older people (especially men past their mid-50s) concentrates employment on the so-called 'prime working years' between 25 and 50 – which are also childrearing years for most women and men.

At the same time enormous economic and technological changes are underway, with major effects on the labour market and people's experience of employment. There is a change from production to consumption as the main focus of the economy. Goods are still manufactured, but the exchange of services and information become ever more important activities. Computers and telecommunications are the defining technologies. The composition and nature of employment is being reconstituted; new types of work based on new skills emerge while others fade away, the information worker versed in new technology replacing the coalminer and steelworker; jobs for life are increasingly a thing of the past, with lifelong learning to re-skill and maintain employability offered in its place; working practices become ever more flexible; the number of women workers increases, while the number of male workers decreases as the day of the male 'breadwinner' passes.

Some see such changes as amounting to a major shift, from industrial to post-industrial or knowledge societies, in which diversity, differentiation and fragmentation replace homogeneity, standardisation and the economies and organisation of scale. Some have gone so far as to define these shifts as revolutionary in nature. Andersson and Sylwans (1997), for example, describe current economic and technological changes as a transformatory process or 'logistic revolution', the fourth such revolution in a series beginning in the thirteenth century. Each revolution has been defined by profound changes in the organisation of production, services, capital and information. The revolution we are living through today, they suggest, is characterised by an extreme complexity which requires non-hierarchical network relationships, new competencies and high levels of creativity, in sharp contrast to the routinisation, standardisation, predictability and authoritarianism which marked the preceding Industrial Revolution.

These developments are related to complex and interrelated economic and political changes since the 1970s, including the increasing dominance of a deregulated global capitalism, greater priority given to competition, markets and profitability, and an enhanced search for profit without regard to national boundaries (a change characterised by Harvey (1989) as a transition from a Fordist capitalism of standardised mass production to a capitalism of 'flexible accumulation'); and a weakening of the nation state which, unable to control the movement of capital and faced by ever more powerful transnational corporations, has adopted an increasingly managerial role to entice roving capital to invest by providing profitable conditions – including a competitive and flexible workforce, both now and for the future.

Such changes have enormous implications for parenting, starting with the most fundamental issues – whether to parent at all, if so when to start (the average age of having a first child is now well over 25) and how many children to bring in to the world (the birth rates in all European countries are below the level needed simply to reproduce the current population). Yet, as a society we have hardly begun the critical analysis of the relationship between employment and parenting and the consequences for this relationship of the changes occurring in the world of paid work. Instead, we shelter behind comforting but bland discussions about 'family friendly' work practices, seeking easy answers before we have found the difficult questions. Organisations concerned with families and parenting (and increasingly government itself) talk about the need for such 'family friendly' practices without questioning how far they do or can address the 'wicked issues' at the heart of the relationship between parenting and employment – in particular time, gender and the compatibility between demands of paid work and caring.

Analysis of the working hours of employed parents between 1984 and 1997 shows a substantial increase amongst employed British mothers (by three hours per week on average), without any corresponding decrease amongst employed fathers who already work the longest hours in Europe, averaging a 47 hour week in 1997 (Holtermann *et al.*, in press). So, while we have had increasing talk, even action, over 'family friendly' policies, this has been against a harsh background of parents' work intensifying (at least as measured in terms of working hours; we have no evidence to substantiate an impression that work may be intensifying in other ways, as employers seek to increase productivity). A similar picture has been presented by Hochschild (1997) in her case study of an American corporation – *The Time Bind* – which shows parents, both mothers and fathers, increasing their hours in the workplace even when family friendly policies are available to them. Moreover, she suggests that they do so in order to escape from the pressures of home and family life.

While there is evidence of fathers taking a somewhat greater share of childcare responsibility and work (Deven *et al.* 1998), in general there has not yet been a major reallocation of family responsibilities in two parent families despite increasing maternal employment. Indeed, it is striking that, as just noted, fathers' working hours in the UK have not fallen as mothers' working hours have increased. To manage the work-family relationship, dual earner families still tend to rely either on the mother working part time hours (and although recent years have seen full-time maternal employment increasing faster than part-time, most employed mothers still work part-time (Holtermann *et al.* in press)), or on their ability to purchase private services together with the low cost of these services which are mainly based on poorly paid women workers.

In his recent book *Corrosion of Character*, Sennett (1998) argues that changes in the nature of employment in the 'new capitalism' are having major personal consequences for workers, their families and communities. Modern workplaces are increasingly characterised by 'short time-frames': people work on short-term projects, change jobs or their jobs change on them, have fleeting associations, then move on:

> It is the time dimension of the new capitalism, rather than hi-tech data transmission, global stock markets or free trade, that most directly affects people's emotional lives outside the workplace. Transposed to the family realm, 'no long term' means keep moving, don't commit yourself and don't sacrifice... This conflict between family and work poses some new questions about adult experience itself. How can long-term purposes be pursued in a short-term society? How can durable social relations be sustained? How can a human being develop a narrative of identity and life history in a society composed of episodes and fragments? (p.27)

Yet despite such troubling questions, and despite widespread awareness of the pace of employment change, recent literature reviews report little work undertaken on the relationship between employment change, parenting or any other aspects of family life (see Brannen *et al.* 1994, Deven *et al.* 1998). In its recent consultative paper *Supporting Families* (Ministerial Group on the Family 1998), the Government emphasises the importance it attaches to stability and security for children – but in the context of lone parenting and the need 'to strengthen the institution of marriage', and without any discussion or analysis of the implications of employment for stability and security.

Whilst these time and gender issues remain fraught, and the implications for family relations of new ways of working are largely ignored, there is an increasing public discussion about the need for 'parents' to be more involved with their children, both in the home and in the services that their children attend, and to devote more time in general to issues of parenthood. This raises a number of as yet unanswered questions – apart from the obvious one of why parenting is receiving so much attention at this particular time. If 'parental involvement' for most of the postwar years was in fact premised on time supplied by mothers who were not employed or worked only very few hours, on what is 'parental involvement' now premised as more parents are employed and work longer hours?

Will parenting education and support increasingly become the preserve of parents outside the labour market, while parents who are heavily engaged in employment minimise their involvement both in direct parenting and in activities aimed at parents? What do we actually know about the relationship between parental involvement in its various forms, and the gender, labour market involvement and occupational status of parents?

What state are we in?

The preceding introduction sets the scene for three points about parenthood and policies and practices to support parenting. First, and most obviously, it seems to me that it is necessary to relate our discussion, policy and practices about parenthood to a continuous, wide-ranging and searching analysis of the world we live in, including the actual relationships of parents to the labour market and, more generally, the nature of employment and capitalism (which I use here as shorthand to describe the dominant form of economic relationships and production in most parts of the world, constituting 'a constantly revolutionary force in world history, a force that perpetually re-shapes the world into new and often quite unexpected configurations' (Harvey 1989, p.186)). We need to know what is happening in employment – again both in general and with respect to parents – and why it may be happening; we need to describe the pace and nature of change; and we need to understand the consequences of change for family life and caring, including parenting. In short, we need to ensure that we contextualise parenthood and parenting in relation to the potent influences of employment and the economy.

Not to do so is naive. Being naive, it may reduce parenting interventions to ineffectiveness and irrelevance, or limit their focus to particular sub-groups leaving such interventions open to the accusation that they are more concerned with issues of normalisation and control than enhancing opportunities and justice. An obvious starting point would be for one location in Government to assume responsibility for the relationship between employment and family life, and for taking a leadership role in deepening our understanding of what is going on. But the issue – understanding the relationship between parenthood and employment, between production and reproduction – cannot be left to Government. It must be a concern of all organisations and all practitioners engaged in work with parents.

A politics of parenthood and a politics of childhood

Second, I would argue that we need to locate the concept and practice of parenting support within a wider context: the development of a 'politics of parenthood' (or, perhaps more broadly, a 'politics of caring'). A politics of parenthood arises from viewing parents as a social group with some common needs and interests (as well as many differences), a social group which needs to be the subject of public dialogue and action. A central subject of this politics is the relationship between reproduction and production, between the social and the economic.

This is always contested territory, a relationship of tensions. Nor will some magic formula remove these tensions. There never was a golden age of reconciliation in the past, nor does one beckon for the future. However, if the contested nature of the relationship is unmasked and recognised, then at least it becomes possible to subject it to critical discussion, drawing on analyses of the world we live in together with the actual experiences of parents struggling to combine employment with childrearing.

The history of the industrial era can be seen as a process of social forces attempting to impose some constraints on the economic forces of capitalism, seeking some compromise between capitalism's enormous but potentially disruptive economic dynamism and the other needs of life, social, environmental, cultural and so on. Since the late 1970s, a new phase of capitalism has emerged; the declining power of organised labour movements, the collapse of Communism and the weakening of the nation state have removed several constraints. The consequences have been global deregulation, the growing reach of the Anglo-American free market, increasing economic inequality, insecurity and volatility, and a dominance of business values and culture – in short the clear ascendency of a politics of production driven by the business values of productivity, profitability, competition and individualism.

A recognised and vigorous 'politics of parenthood' could play an important part in the process of re-establishing a new balance, including the search for new means to constrain capitalism and bring it into a new relationship with non-economic human needs. This 'politics of parenthood' will need to find critical questions to set a new public agenda, as well as finding fora where these questions can be identified, refined and debated and which enable parents and others to organise to take action – fora that are public spaces 'where people come together to speak, to engage in dialogue, to share their stories and to struggle together within social relations that strengthen rather than weaken possibilities for active citizenship' (Giroux 1989, p.201).

Giroux, in the preceding quotation, is referring to the possibility of schools being such public spaces. Other possible candidates for providing fora for a 'politics of parenthood' are early childhood institutions (nurseries and other centres taking children below school age). This means understanding these institutions in a particular way, as *public fora situated in civil society in which children and adults participate together in projects of social, cultural, political and economic significance.* One of these projects could be the promotion of an informed, participatory and critical local democracy, with burgeoning community institutions such as nurseries providing new possibilities for the practice of democracy and the development of new social movements addressing important subjects that have so far been inadequately served by traditional political institutions, notably Parliament and local government.

One of these subjects needs to be the responsibilities of women and men in the care and upbringing of children, addressed in relation to the larger subject of the relationship between employment and caring for children:

> At the same time that they provide care and enable parents to participate in the labour market, early childhood institutions can also provide opportunities for the relationship between employment and caring for children to be problematised and debated, through children and adults – including parents, politicians, employers and trade unionists – engaging in critical dialogue based on actual practice and experience. In this way, the early childhood institution can avoid an unquestioning collusion with the demands of the labour market, however unsympathetic to parenting these demands may be, and resist the mechanistic role of simply ensuring an adequate supply of labour. Instead, it can become a space for democratic debate and deepening understanding about the important subject of the relationship between production and reproduction and, more generally, between employment and life in general (Dahlberg *et al.* 1999, p.78)

Equally important, early childhood institutions can provide fora in civil society for *constructing a new public discourse about early childhood* itself, an important part of what might be called a 'politics of childhood'. For early childhood institutions are an obvious place for the public discussion of issues such as pedagogical work and questions such as, how do we understand early childhood? what is our construction of the young child? what is the relationship between young children and society? Another subject for a politics of childhood may be called *issues of the 'good life'*. In the case of early childhood institutions, 'good life' questions might include 'what do we want for our children?' and 'what is a good childhood?'. By using the term 'good life' I do not assume that there is one true 'good life' to be discovered and lived, one conception of the good life that will prove equally acceptable to all. There may well be many in a plural democracy. The point is however that the early childhood institution as forum provides opportunities to enter into dialogue with others about 'good life' issues.

Early childhood institutions, or indeed other places with the potential for conducting a 'politics of parenthood' as well as a 'politics of childhood', are not intrinsically fora. Indeed the purposes of early childhood institutions are not self-evident. These institutions can be many things and we have choices to make about what we want them to be. To take extreme examples, we can understand early childhood institutions simply as places to ensure an adequate supply of labour – nurseries as producers of 'childcare' – or we can understand them as fora which have *inter alia* an overtly political purpose.

Who do we think we are parenting?

The final point concerning parenthood that I want to make in this chapter again arises from changes in the labour market and employment. The reduced availability of parental care and the increased use of non-parental care throws into sharp relief the question of the relationship between children, parents and society. At this point, before going further, I need to raise the issue of who we think the child is – because again, like the purpose of early childhood institutions, the answer is not self-evident.

In recent years there has been increasing questioning about childhood and who the young child is and might be. In particular the idea of a universal child, an essential child, a child objectively knowable irrespective of time or place, context or perspective has been questioned, as has the discipline which has sought to define and identify this child. Developmental psychology has been going through an extended process of problematisation, both from without the discipline but also from within and including some of the most well-known names in the discipline (see Bronfenbrenner *et al.* 1986, Burman 1994, Cole 1996, Elder *et al.* 1993, Henriques *et al.* 1984, Kessel and Siegel 1983, Kessen 1979, Lubeck 1996, Mayall 1996, Morss 1996, Prout and James 1998, Walkerdine 1984). Questions have been asked about the discipline's positivist approach and methods, including the reduction of complexity to simplified and quantifiable representations, and its suspicion, even rejection, of subjectivity and philosophy; its belief in general laws and universal truths, personified by the decontextualised view of development as a biologically-determined sequence of stages; its focus on the individual as the centrepiece of enquiry; a strong normalising tendency; its implication in processes of regulation and control; and the very concept of 'development' itself.

There has been a growing interest in the idea of many and diverse childhoods, related to particular temporal and spatial contexts, and constructed by adults and children themselves through discourse:

the social institution of childhood [is] an actively negotiated set of social relationships within which the early years of human life are constituted. The immaturity of children is a biological fact; but the ways in which this immaturity is understood and made meaningful is a fact of culture. It is these 'facts of culture' which may vary, and which can be said to make childhood a social institution... Childhood is both constructed and reconstructed both for and by children (Prout and James 1997, p.7)

One of the implications of this analysis is that parenthood is not a process of finding out *the* truth about childhood and about how children develop and what their needs are. Rather it is a process of producing understandings and images, of choosing how to see the child. Parents do not do this in a vacuum. Constructions of child-hood are widely influenced by powerful discourses, including the knowledge claims of experts and ideological claims of politicians and the media.

I have argued elsewhere (Moss and Petrie 1997) that the con-struction of the child in Britain is dominated by two ideas or images. The first of these widespread and influential ideas about children can be illustrated if we consider how children usually make the news. Look at the newspapers any week and see how children are represented: as the subjects of abuse or the perpetrators of crimes, as failing pupils or unruly nuisances. Look too at the pervasive and unproblematised use of terms like 'children in need', not only in legislation and service delivery, but in media events and fund-raising.

These representations construct the child as poor, weak and innocent, or as primitive, uncontrollable and threatening. Although apparently opposites, both of these constructions draw on ideas about the child as nature or as a *tabula rasa*, starting with and from nothing, *becoming* a realised, socialised and adult human being. The metaphor for *childhood* is a ladder of development, from in-completeness to maturity, climbing out of childhood into adulthood; while the metaphor for the *child* is an initially empty vessel, to be filled over time with knowledge, identity and correct values poured in by adults – the young child as re-producer.

The second dominant idea is that children are considered to be primarily the private responsibility of parents or, to be precise, of mothers; in our society, we still view the care of children as mainly women's work even now that most mothers are employed. The child–parent relationship becomes more prominent as the welfare state gradually retreats and welfare becomes increasingly privatised and marketised, a process that has been prominent in the early childhood field over the last 15 years. This process has particularly problematic consequences for children, since they are unable to take full responsibility for their own welfare, exposing them to the full forces of the market with its inherent inequalities and insecurities.

To sum up, the second dominant idea constructs children as dependent and privatised, as being in relationship to the family, and in strongly individualistic terms – but neither as a member of a social group nor in relation to society. As a society we seem very confident in talking about the relationship between the child and his or her parents within the nuclear family; indeed we often talk about it in a decontextualised way as if it was autonomous, occurring independent of other relationships and outside society. When it comes to other relationships, for example between children and other children or between children and society, or more broadly, between children, parents and society, we are much less certain: in fact, I would argue that there is no clear understanding of these relationships, nor of children as a social group in society.

These constructions are problematic both from the perspective of the child – for they produce an image of the 'poor' child – and of parents, in particular mothers – for they normalise full-time maternal care. The young child is understood as biologically determined to need exclusive maternal care, certainly in his or her earliest years (up to around the age of three years), with a gradual introduction thereafter into the company of other children and adults. The mother is biologically determined to provide such care. Not to receive or to give this exclusive care is unnatural and harmful, undermining the young child's attachment to his or her mother and exposing the young child to relationships with other adults and children for which he or she is unready. To illustrate the continuing power of these constructions, a large survey undertaken in the European Union in 1993 reported that more than three quarters of all respondents thought that mothers should stay at home when children are young (Malpas and Lambert 1993).

These constructions of childhood and motherhood produce enormous tensions and anxieties at a time of labour market change leading to increased numbers of employed parents, in particular mothers who are closing the employment gap with fathers even if they still have some way to go. Non-maternal care is understood as either wholly bad or, at best, an inferior *substitute* for the real thing. Unequipped to envisage alternative childhoods, employed parents seek a very particular concept of care: to provide a substitute home reproducing, as closely as possible, the model of maternal care. This is sought either through individualised forms of care (for example, family day carers, nannies or relatives); or through the organisation of early childhood institutions and the structuring of relationships between children and staff in these institutions, with importance attached to high ratios of staff to children and the need for close, intimate and cosy relationships between staff and children (Penn 1997, Dahlberg *et al.* 1999). In this way, the early childhood institution is constructed not only as a producer of childcare but as a substitute home, the workers as substitute mothers.

There are, however, other constructions of early childhood, constructions which envisage a very different idea of who the young child is and which produce different understandings of the purposes of early childhood institutions and, more broadly, of the relationship between the child, his or her parents and society. For example, the young child can be understood and recognised as being a member of society, existing not only in the family home, but also in the wider world outside; as such the young child is a citizen, with citizen's rights and, as he or she is capable of assuming them, citizen's responsibilities. Related to this understanding, the young child can also be seen as a *co-constructor*, from the very start of life, of knowledge and identity, as a unique, complex and individual subject, engaging with and making sense of the world from birth, but *always* doing this in relationship with others, both adults and other children. It is this construction of the young child, of the young child born (in the famous phrase of Loris Malaguzzi) with a hundred languages, that has inspired the pedagogical work in the Italian town of Reggio-Emilia[1]:

> Our image of children no longer considers them as isolated and egocentric, does not see them only engaged in action with objects, does not emphasize only the cognitive aspects, does not belittle feelings or what is not logical and does not consider with ambiguity the role of the affective domain. Instead our image of the child is rich in potential, strong, powerful, competent and, most of all, connected to adults and other children. (Loris Malaguzzi 1993a, p.10)

Understanding the young child as a co-constructor and active participant, wanting and responding to a wide range of relationships, in the home and outside, with other children and adults, we can open up to the possibility for a childhood of many relationships and opportunities, in which *both* the home *and* the early childhood institution have important, complementary but different parts to play. This possibility has been recognised by the children in Reggio Emilia,

> who understood sooner than expected that their adventures in life could flow between two places. [Through early childhood institutions] they could express their previously overlooked desire to be with their peers and find in them points of reference, under-standing, surprises, affective ties and merriment that could dispel shadows and uneasiness. For the children and their families there now opened up the possibility of a very long and continuous period of [children] living together [with each other], 5 or 6 years of reciprocal trust and work. (Malaguzzi 1993b, p.55)

These references to Reggio-Emilia, a city incidentally with very high levels of parental employment, reflect the enormous importance of the experience of early childhood work in this Italian city over the last 35 years. The early childhood institutions in Reggio can be seen as struggling with some of the issues raised in this chapter, in particular the possibility of providing fora for a politics of parenthood and childhood, involving parents, practitioners, politicians and children themselves.

> What is so terribly impressive and exceptional about the Reggio experience and the work of Loris Malaguzzi is the way they have challenged the dominating discourses of our time, specifically in the field of early childhood pedagogy – a most unique undertaking for a pedagogical practice! This was achieved by deconstructing the way in which the field has been socially constituted within a scientific, political and ethical context and then reconstructing and redefining children's and teachers' subjectivities. That is, they have tried to understand what kinds of thoughts, conceptions, ideas, social structures and behavioural patterns have dominated the field and how these discourses have shaped our conceptions and images of the child and childhood, the way we interact with children and the kind of environment we create for them … As I see it, all of this was possible because Malaguzzi was extremely familiar with the field and its traditions; but he also had the courage and originality to choreo-graph his own thinking. (Dahlberg 1995, p.10)

This quotation captures some of the elements of Reggio's practice, understanding and perspective: choosing to adopt a social constructionist approach; challenging and deconstructing dominant discourses, realising the power of these discourses in shaping our thoughts and actions, including the field of early childhood pedagogy; rejecting the prescription of rules, goals, methods and standards, and in so doing risking uncertainty and complexity; having the courage to think for themselves in constructing new discourses, and in so doing daring to make the choice of understanding the child as a rich child, a child of infinite capabilities, a child born with a hundred languages; building a new pedagogical project, fore-grounding relationships and encounters, dialogue and confrontation, reflexion and critical thinking; border crossing disciplines and perspectives, replacing 'either/or' positions with a 'both/and' openness; and an active and enquiring relationship to the major issues of our times – childhood, the environment, peace and human coexistence – as well as to developments in science and philosophy.

In conclusion

In this chapter I have argued that parenthood and childhood are political, as well as social and cultural, issues. They are subjects of value rather than simply products of objective knowledge. They involve philosophical, political and ethical issues, rather than just the managerial transference and application of a 'best practice' technology of objectively determined needs and solutions. They are interwoven into a context which includes economic structures of great power and dynamism, a context both so complex and challenging that it is tempting to ignore, focusing instead on what appears to be more manageable slices of life.

Parenthood and childhood therefore are contested areas, producing a plurality of understandings, each permeated with values. Messy and anxiety provoking certainly. But, I would argue, preferable to a belief in the possibility of describing some universal ideal of the 'good' parent or a 'normal' child – for 'it is in the graveyard of universal consensus that responsibility and freedom and the individual exhale their last sigh' (Bauman 1997, p.202).

This has led me to speculate about the nature of parental support. Rather than seeing support as some foundation for building a 'true' understanding of who children are and what parents should be, support might be understood in an 'emancipatory' sense, enabling people to challenge dominant ideas and discourses and their related power relationships; to gain deeper understanding of the world we live in; to have the courage and capacity to think for themselves; and by so doing, to take more control of their lives. This does not mean creating some kind of revolutionary situation, rather something more modest and attainable, parents developing the ability 'to perceive critically the way they exist in the world with which and in which they find themselves – [and coming] to see the world not as a static reality but as a reality in process, in transformation' (Freire 1985) and practising (in Foucault's words) 'the art of not being governed so much'.

This does not mean there is no scope for policies and practices. In the field of parenthood and employment, for example, there are a range of possibilities which may provide important practical support to parents and improve the lives of parents and children – such as good quality and accessible services for children which provide care as well as other functions, and paid and flexible leave arrangements including parental leave and leave to care for children who are unwell. But these, or any other interventions, never fall out of a clear, blue sky. They are the products of economic forces, political processes and power relationships, dominant discourses and constructions. Parenting support needs to engage with these forces, processes and relationships, and to problematise the discourses and constructions, in short understanding that the parenting relationship extends beyond the parent and child to the extensive network of social and economic relationships within which parent and child are located.

Note

Since the end of the Second World War, the Northern Italian city of Reggio-Emilia has built up an extensive network of early childhood institutions for children from 0 to 6 (attended by 36 per cent of children age 0 to 3 and 98 per cent of children aged 3 to 6 years) and has continually struggled to develop a closely related pedagogical theory and practice. The results have been spectacular, the pedagogical work in Reggio's early childhood institutions becoming the subject of world-wide interest and admiration. This has been a collective achievement of the parents, politicians, practitioners and children of Reggio, but if one name should be singled out it is that of Loris Malaguzzi, the first head of the early childhood service, who died in 1993.

References

Andersson, A. E. and Sylwans, P. (1997) *Framtidens arbete och liv (Work and Life of the Future)*. Stockholm: Natur och Kultur.

Atkinson, D. and Elliott, L. (1998) 'Anxious? Insecure? You can get used to it', *Guardian*, 6 June.

Bauman, Z. (1997) *Postmodernity and its Discontents*. Cambridge: Polity Press.

Brannen, J. and Moss, P. (1998) 'The polarisation and intensification of parental employment in Britain: consequences for children, families and the community', *Community, Work and Family* **1**(3), 229–47.

Brannen, J., Moss, P., Owen, C., Wale, C. (1997) *Mothers, Fathers and Employment: parents and the labour market, 1984–1994* (DfEE Research Report No. 10). London: DfEE.

Brannen, J., Moss, P., Poland, G., Mesaros, G. (1994) *Employment and Family Life: a review of research in the UK 1980–94* (Research Series, No. 41). London: Employment Department.

Bronfenbrenner, U. *et al.* (1986) 'Towards a critical social history of developmental psychology', *American Psychologist* **41** (11), 1218–30

Burman, E. (1994) *Deconstructing Developmental Psychology*. London: Routledge.

Cole, M. (1996) *Cultural Psychology: a once and future discipline*. Cambridge, Mass.: The Belknap Press of Harvard University Press.

Dahlberg. G. (1995) 'Everything is a beginning and everything is dangerous: some reflections on the Reggio Emilia experience'. Paper given at an international seminar *Nostalgio del Futuro* in honour of Loris Malaguzzi, Milan, October 1995.

Dahlberg, G., Moss, P., Pence, A. (1999) *Beyond Quality in Early Childhood Education and Care: postmodern perspectives*. London: Falmer Press.

Deven, F. *et al.* (1998) *State of the Art Review on Reconciliation of Work and Family Responsibilities and Quality in Care Services* (DfEE Research Report No. 57). London: DfEE.

Elder, G., Modell, J., Parke, R. (eds) (1993) *Children in Time and Place*. Cambridge: Cambridge University Press.

Freire, P. (1985 English edition) *Pedagogy of the Oppressed*. Harmondsworth: Penguin Books.

Giroux, H. (1989) *Schooling for Democracy: critical pedagogy in the modern age*. London: Routledge.

Harvey, D. (1989) *The Condition of Postmodernity*. Oxford: Blackwells.

Henriques, J. *et al.* (1984) *Changing the Subject: psychology, Social regulation and subjectivity*. London: Methuen.

Hochschild, A. (1997) *The Time Bind: when work becomes home and home becomes work*. New York: Metropolitan Books.

Hodgkin, R. and Newell, P. (1996) *Effective Government Structures for Children*. London: the Calouste Gulbenkian Foundation.

Holtermann, S., Brannen, J., Moss, P., Owen. C. (in press) *Lone Parents and the Labour Market*. Sheffield: Employment Service.

Hutton, W. (1995) *The State We Are In*. London: Jonathan Cape.

Kessen, W. (1979) 'The American child and other cultural inventions'. *American Psychologist* **24**, 815–20.

Kessen, W. (1983) 'The child and other cultural inventions', in Kessel, F. and Siegel, A. (eds) *The Child and other Cultural Inventions: Houston Symposium 4*. New York: Praeger.

Lubeck, S. (1996) 'Deconstructing "Child Development Knowledge" and "Teacher Preparation"', *Early Childhood Research Quarterly* **11**, 147–67.

Malaguzzi, L. (1993a) 'For an education based on relationships'. *Young Children*, November, 9–13.

Malaguzzi, L. (1993b) 'History. ideas and basic philosophy', in Edwards, C., Gandini, L., Forman, G. (eds) *The Hundred Languages of Children*. Norwood, NJ: Ablex.

Malpas, N. and Lambert, P-Y. (1993) *The Europeans and the Family; results of an opinion survey (Eurobarometer 39)*. Brussels: European Commission.

Mayall, B. (1996) *Children, Health and the Social Order*. Buckingham: Open University Press.

Ministerial Group on the Family (1998) *Supporting Families*. London: Stationery Office.

Morss, J. (1996) *Growing Critical*. London: Routledge.

Moss, P. and Petrie, P. (1997) *Children's Services: time for a new approach*. London: Institute of Education University of London.

Penn, H. (1997) *Comparing Nurseries*. London: Paul Chapman Publishing.

Prout, A. and James, A. (1997) 'A new paradigm for the sociology of childhood?', in James, A. and Prout, A. (eds) *Constructing and Deconstructing Childhood: Contemporary Issues in the sociological study of childhood*, 2nd edn. London: Falmer Press.

Sennett, R. (1998) *Corrosion of Character: The personal consequences of work in the new capitalism*. London: Norton.

Walkerdine, V. (1984) 'Developmental psychology and the child-centred pedagogy: the insertion of Piaget into early education', in Henriques, J. *et al. Changing the Subject: psychology, social regulation and subjectivity*. London: Methuen.

Chapter 7

The emotional education of parents: attachment theory and emotional literacy

James Park

Introduction

Recent research in attachment theory indicates that providing parents
with opportunities to develop their understanding of the feelings
they experience within relationships can help to enhance the
sensitivity with which they respond to their children's emotional
needs. Whilst the time of preparation for, and initiation into,
parenting provides a particularly good opportunity to shift
preconceptions about personal history, there can be a substantial
time-lag between the beginning of any programme and significant
enhancement of interactions between parent and child. Focused
parenting programmes can have a more powerful impact if they are
complemented by a broader strategy for enabling individuals
throughout the population to develop the qualities associated with
'emotional literacy' – including an ability to recognise their own
feelings, to read the emotional responses of others, and to deploy
these combined understandings in the development of positive
relationships. The benefits of such a strategy could be supported by,
and bring benefits to, the workplace as well as the community.

Various factors have influenced the level of interest currently being
taken in parenting programmes. Amongst these is an increased
understanding of the impact that interactions between children and
caregivers have on individuals' capacity to develop their emotional
and social skills, and to make positive use of the opportunities that
become available to them throughout life.

Much of this new understanding comes from research in
attachment theory, which has led to the development of systematic
frameworks for linking the experience that children have of carers
to their potential for optimal development (Bowlby 1988, Holmes
1993). Attachment theory is used to support the argument presented
in this chapter.

The theory makes links between the capacity of parents to be
available and responsive to the emotional needs of others and their

children's ability to construct healthy relationships, develop a positive outlook on life and achieve a significant measure of personal fulfilment (Main *et al.* 1985)

Additionally, it shows how the care that parents provide for their children is likely to reflect patterns in their own experience of being parented, and draws attention to the processes that make it possible for negative elements in such patterns to give way to responses that are more likely to promote the development of emotionally healthy children (Main and Hesse 1990).

By demonstrating that there is scope for ameliorating the response patterns that potentially impair children's development, research into attachment makes a strong argument for parenting programmes. By also demonstrating how difficult it is to do so within a limited time frame, and to what extent unsatisfactory attachment experiences in childhood can limit the life chances of individuals (Simpson and Rhodes 1994, Hinde and Schwarz 1994), research further argues that parenting programmes need to be supported by a comprehensive strategy to develop 'emotional literacy' in the population. After looking at the lessons to be drawn from attachment theory, this chapter addresses the issue of what such a strategy might comprise.

Attachment and parenting

The parental task is to find ways of ensuring that children are sufficiently able to satisfy their instinctive needs so as to ensure that they can go on to realise some of their potential, and to become over the course of time adults capable of living in ways that are relatively purposeful and fulfilling.

Attachment theory was developed by John Bowlby as a challenge to the viewpoint held by British psychoanalysts during the 1930s that infants sought relationships with adults only in order to satisfy their physical need for warmth, food and shelter. Bowlby's argument was that the seeking-out of the attentions of a parent was a hard-wired part of the instinctive system with which children were born, and was independent of those other needs. Within this theory, even infants who are kept warm and nourished will only thrive if they also receive attention from carers who are capable of responding appropriately to the sounds, gestures and silences through which they seek to indicate their needs.

Infants require such attention from caregivers because it is only when an intimate other is available to regulate their emotional states that they will be sufficiently free from anxiety to explore the world into which they are born, to learn their own ways of managing the emotions that the changing environment provokes in them and to find out how they can have an influence on their surroundings.

Infants do not know that they are persons, that the reflex reactions of arms, legs and mouth belong to them, that all people have feelings which are sometimes pleasurable and sometimes unpleasant (Mahler *et al.* 1975). Nor do they have any way of distinguishing inner experience from outer sensation, people from objects. Only slowly can they start to make sense of the world around them, of the things that are being done to them, and of the actions they are capable of carrying out. It is the presence of the parent or carer that makes it possible for infants to absorb and process that information, then to learn ways of thinking about it.

The emotional educator

The role of caregivers, in this account, is to provide children with an interactive sounding board against which they can come to know themselves, other people and the nature of the wider world into which they have been born. They do so initially through their attempts to understand the messages that infants convey about the sensations to which they are exposed, to communicate these attempts at understanding back to their infants and to assuage, through their attentive and soothing presence, the undefined anxieties created by the infant's roller-coaster ride through the primary experiences of cold, heat, hunger, thirst, touch and other sensations.

The child psychiatrist Donald Winnicott described this process as being about 'giving back to the baby the baby's own self' (Winnicott 1967). This involves the parent acting as an extension of a baby's self for long enough to enable that baby to start the process of discovering that their own self is distinct from anyone else's, and what that might mean. It is about staying with the child through the process of continuously rediscovering, at each stage of the developmental process, that he or she has a distinct self, one that is capable of defining and carrying through personal objectives. It is about allowing oneself to be used as a source of emotional succour so that one's children can manage the feelings aroused by their changing awareness of the world and the part they play in it.

Through analysing video recordings of interactions between caregivers and their children, Daniel Stern has demonstrated how intense is the sequence of exchanges through which the parental task is performed. Carer and child are locked into a continuous series of 'very small, ordinary, daily, repetitive nonverbal events', that reflect the carer's 'wishes, fears and fantasies' about the infant, and which become the 'building blocks of the representational world' for the infant (Stern 1995).

Through this exchange of gestures, sounds and acts, the caregiver enables the child to understand and to tolerate the feelings they are having. By rendering the emotions relatively unthreatening, they open up space for exploration of the context within which these feeling states happen. The child develops the ability both to be 'reflective' about emotions in general, and to use the knowledge of self and other that they have gleaned to become engaged with all the other questions about the world that come up for them. The more 'secure' children feel in the relationship with their carers, the more likely they are to be comfortable with their own feelings and those of other people. Their inner security enables them to develop the ability to access, understand and respond appropriately to a wide range of emotional experience in themselves and in others (Fonagy *et al.* 1995).

Parents can only make those feelings of love, hate, remorse, guilt and shame tolerable to the child by displaying their own capacity to tolerate them. Through interactions of this sort, carers teach their children that it is possible to manage and endure feelings that might otherwise be experienced as overwhelming. In this way, parents set up boundaries around these powerful feeling states, enabling children to access the many dimensions of who they are, and to use their feelings as guides to thinking and acting. The alternative is for the child to seek out ways of protecting themselves from feelings that are experienced as dangerous and threatening (Sroufe 1990).

Parental sensitivity

To act as a parent in this way requires one to have some capacity to empathise with the feelings of one's children, and to tolerate the vicissitudes of their emotional needs – which may manifest alternately as clinginess, assertiveness or recalcitrance. The carer needs to show that he or she can grasp some of what the child is feeling, and can return those feelings in ways that make them somewhat more intelligible. Their pattern of responsiveness – communicated by physical gestures, sounds and actions – needs to be sufficiently stable and predictable for it to be somewhat understood – reassuring the child that he or she can place trust in the person who has taken on responsibility for him or her. The child is acutely sensitive to any shift in the emotional message contained in this sequence of responses. He or she will quickly register any mismatch between the response expected and that which is actually received – whether as a result of distraction, depression or some other cause (Murray *et al.* 1993).

By being able to recognise that the child has distinct feeling experiences, and by responding in appropriate ways to those feelings, parents make it possible for their children to take a real interest in the mental states of others, to start thinking about where these mental states come from, and what the relationship is between the feelings they experience and those experienced by others. Children who know enough about their own emotions to engage meaningfully with others have enormous opportunities to enhance their learning through social interaction. They grow up with a base of self-confidence upon which to build. They become capable of setting goals for their lives and of engaging meaningfully with others.

Where, by contrast, the parent is unable to engage in such sensitive interactions, the child is left prey to emotions that they cannot manage except defensively. If this experience of abandonment is further compounded by the parent behaving in ways that apply additional emotional pressure – by disconfirming the child's perception of an event, refusing their calls for comfort or invalidating their subjective experience of what is happening to them – these responses will either intensify existing emotional states, or provoke new states that are equally hard for the child to manage (Marrone 1998).

Recent neurobiological research has deepened our understanding of why it is so deeply damaging for a child to be subjected to emotional stress without any prospect of relief. Infants who are left in states of emotional hyperarousal – whether through exposure to sources of intense stress or through the absence of a carer figure to soothe anxiety – experience significant distortions of cerebral development (Perry 1995). The perpetuation of an anxious state keeps the panic response open for so long that it becomes highly sensitised, and subsequently requires only a minor stimulus to set it off again. Those to whom this has happened will tend to operate in a condition of continuous high-alert, always on the lookout for threats and dangers, unable to concentrate on anything else that is happening.

There are various ways in which children respond to the cascade of overwhelming emotions provoked by, or compounded by, the absence or inadequacy of the parental figure. They may learn to cut themselves off from exposure to feelings and to deny their need for contact with others. Others will adopt compliant stances expressive of their neediness. And others will become emotionally disorganised, and respond to other people in dysfunctional ways. Attachment theory describes these groups as, respectively, Avoidant, Ambivalent and Chaotic (Holmes 1993).

From child to parent

These experiences of our carers provide all of us with a template through which we perceive ourselves. Bowlby described how children built up 'working models' of how attachment figures were likely to behave towards them in different situations; and shaped around these their expectations of others (Bowlby 1973). These patterns of thinking about self and other have a strong tendency to persist into later life, and to shape the behaviours that people adopt in relationships – whether with partners or with children (Marris 1996).

It is because these working models are so adhesive that they impact so significantly upon the ability of individuals to provide appropriate responses to their children when they, in turn, become parents. They bring to their parenting not only their characteristic patterns of feeling, as they have been constructed out of the interaction between their attachment history and their current socio-economic situation, but also the feelings evoked in them by their children. Exposure to the experiences of their children act to remind them of their own childhoods, affecting the way in which they display anger, irritability, sadness, anxiety and other emotions.

Parents who were not helped to tolerate certain feelings in their own infancy and childhood, and have not developed effective strategies for doing so in later life, will find it difficult to fully experience those same feelings in their children. They will either not hear what is being communicated, or they will misunderstand it, and will tend as a result to respond in inappropriate ways that the child finds frustrating, confusing or distressing (Fonagy 1998). The response of the child to the mother's inadvertent emotional neglect often brings further reminders of unsatisfactory interactions, deepening the mother's feelings of anger or despair, and intensifying the negative cycle (Brown 1982, Radke-Yarrow 1991).

Attachment researchers seeking to elucidate how these processes work start by eliciting from parents an understanding of their own ability to handle emotions (by analysing the narrative style with which they recount specific incidents in their childhood and the feelings they associate with them), and then correlating this information with findings about the attachment patterns of their children. In this way, they have shown that the attachment classification of the parent, as established during the pregnancy, is highly predictive of the later attachment classification of the child (Main *et al.* 1985). The parents, in short, are likely to offer their own children an experience of being parented that is of the same quality as their own was (Main and Hesse 1990).

The emotionally secure parent can give an account of their childhood experiences, and of what they observed of the relationships between their parents, that is coherent, consistent and basically credible. Their narrative accounts are convincing and well-organised, characterised by 'a free-flowing, spontaneous style of discourse, a relative absence of self-deception, the acceptance of the need to depend on others, and an ease with imperfections in both self and parents' (Steele and Steele 1994, p.103). These qualities help them in attending to the emotional needs of their children.

By contrast, when adults who have developed insecure attachment patterns are asked about their emotional experiences, they will tend to dismiss them or to direct the discussion elsewhere, revealing their inability to communicate what they are feeling. By tuning out from their own inner experience in this way, they limit also their ability to understand what their children are undergoing. They are also unable to expose themselves to experiences or thoughts that may stimulate these hard-to-endure feelings. As a result, they cannot hear what their children are attempting to communicate.

Shifting the pattern

In order to effect, and sustain, an improvement in parents' ability to respond sensitively and appropriately to the needs of their children, there is a need to find ways of helping them to more fully experience their own emotions. In her research into 'ghosts in the nursery', Selma Fraiberg drew attention to the distinction between those parents who could give a *factual* account of any traumatic, difficult or painful experiences they had endured in their childhoods, and those who were also able to get in touch with the powerful *feelings* that were evoked by these experiences (Fraiberg 1987). It was the ability to give an account that encompassed both the cognitive and the affective dimensions of what they had gone through which enabled them to connect to what their own children were experiencing. This created an ability to provide the sensitivity and responsiveness that their children needed in order for them to flourish.

What, though, enables parents to find ways of changing their representations of themselves in relation to others? A number of parenting projects work on the principle that the emotions generated by pregnancy need to be shared by parents in conditions of emotional security. The Early Years project in the Shankill area of Belfast, for example, not only provides parents with the support of a project worker, but also operates two operational centres where families can meet each other and share experiences. The Dawn Project in South Yorkshire sees the courses it offers to adults and children recovering from the trauma of divorce and separation as a springboard to the development of mutual support groups.

This is taken further by projects such as PIPPIN, based in Hertfordshire, which brings together mothers and fathers during the third trimester of pregnancy, and seeks to provide them with the sort of 'secure base' that was not sufficiently available to them in their childhood, and is not present in their current social relationships. This provides a non-judgemental context within which they can explore themselves in relation to other people, play out patterns of behaviour in ways that help them to learn more about the emotional states that give rise to them, deal with the issues that provoke strong feelings in them, and through this often painful process can come to better understand what are appropriate responses to their children in any particular situation (Pound 1990).

One survey of research carried out into American parenting programmes that aimed to change insecure attachment patterns into secure ones describes how difficult this goal is to achieve. It showed not only that many projects which were apparently effective in changing parental behaviour had little impact on infant security, but it also described projects where changes in the self-understanding of parents initially impacted negatively on the attachment patterns of their children. In the case of one project aimed at mothers who were at high risk because of poverty, lack of education, and social isolation, the infants of only 46 per cent of participants were securely attached at 12 months, as opposed to 67 per cent of the controls. The authors claim that this may have been due to the amount of time that changes in the representations of the mother take to impact upon the behaviour of the child, and they back this claim with reference to a case study that tracked the application of two therapeutic modalities in treating a depressed mother and her two-month-old son. At 12 months, the level of maternal sensitivity continued to be low, and the quality of the attachment relationship remained insecure. At 18 months, the mother began to show more sensitivity and less intrusiveness. At 20 months, the attachment relationship had been transformed in a positive direction (Van Ijzendoorn *et al.* 1995)

Promoting emotional literacy

Given the difficulties involved in achieving an improvement in parental sensitivity that will impact on the child's emotional development, the amount of time that may elapse before any intervention has a benefit for the child, and the general need for emotional sensitivity in interpersonal relationships, there would seem to be a clear case for looking at ways of enhancing the 'emotional literacy' – the ability to recognise their own feelings and to read the emotional responses of others – of prospective parents *before* they are confronted with the challenge of caring for their children. This could also lead to an enhancement in the ability of individuals to engage in meaningful learning, to form stable and satisfying relationships, to work collaboratively with others and to engage positively in the life of their communities.

To achieve such a goal would require the provision of multiple opportunities for individuals to develop forms of self-understanding that they can deploy in their own lives and in their relationships with other people. The PIPPIN model referred to above suggests that the way to achieve this is through providing people with contexts that are experienced as emotionally safe, in which they can speak freely about their own experiences, and can hear others speak equally freely about their own. The group process provides a 'container' for the difficult feelings that people experience, allowing them to rise to the surface and to be examined. They can learn to create a coherent and consistent narrative account of crucial events in their own lives.

Emotional literacy through education

An obvious place to start the work of developing such qualities is within the school system. This would involve enabling young people to explore their own emotional histories and experiences alongside, and as part of, the academic curriculum. A learning approach which had emotional literacy as a goal would look for ways of enabling students to make connections between their knowledge of themselves and the values they believe in, the ideas which resonate for them and the actions which can make their lives meaningful. By enabling them to establish links between their inner worlds and their outer experience, it would provide young people with new ways of finding the motivation they need to reach out and grasp for diverse forms of knowledge, and to experiment with creative solutions to the challenges that confront them, both as individuals and as members of society.

Currently, there are a range of projects within schools which provide young people with opportunities to achieve these aims. The Developmental Groupwork approach developed by Leslie Button in the 1970s (Thacker *et al.* 1992) has much in common with the styles of Circle Time developed by Jenny Mosley in Wiltshire (Mosley 1996), Murray White in Cambridge (White 1992) and by other teachers in classrooms around the country. The principle of creating structures that provide sufficient safety for emotional exploration to begin are central also to programmes for peer mediation, anger management, conflict resolution and violence reduction, as delivered by organisations such as the National Coalition Building Institute in Leicester[1] or Conflict and Change in East Ham.[2] These approaches differ both in the nature of the strategies they adopt to ensure that young people feel safe enough to explore their emotions, and in the degree to which open expression is controlled as a guarantor of safety (Antidote 1998).

The effectiveness of such programmes is likely to be limited by the extent to which the school as a whole organisation provides children and young people with an overall context of emotional safety. Where powerful emotions are evoked by the way a school is run, and by interactions between pupils, or between pupils and staff, and these have no outlet other than an occasional slot in the curriculum, it is unlikely that whatever groupwork process is on offer can do more than provide an occasional outlet for feelings and a glimpse at the possibility of emotional understanding.

A different approach is required if schools are to fulfil their potential for providing children and young people with an emotional education that not only supports their learning, but also enhances their opportunities to live fulfilling lives. Such an approach would recognise that the feeling individual needs to be put at the centre of whatever is being studied, or whatever other activities are taking place in the school, rather than outside it. This would involve recognising that:

- Emotional learning is a valuable component in any academic subject, not only the arts, but science and technology subjects too.
- High-quality teaching can only happen in the context of strong and positive relationships between teachers and their pupils.
- Teachers need to have their own emotions recognised and met so that they can respond appropriately to those of their pupils.
- Children and young people will only develop a sense of commitment to their schools if they are consulted about what they learn, how they learn and how the school is run.
- Schools will become more effective if they see themselves as community learning centres for learners of all ages (Bentley 1998).
- The diversity of talents and skills that children and young people have need to be recognised and valued through the processes of inspection and validation that go on within schools (Antidote 1997).

Emotions at work

Experiences in the workplace also have the potential to enhance or diminish the potential of individuals to develop the qualities associated with emotional literacy. The interpersonal situations experienced there may either be opportunities for people to learn more about themselves and others, or to replay dysfunctional patterns developed in childhood. Where the workplace evokes high levels of stress, and provides insufficient opportunities for individuals to enhance the management of their emotional responses, the effect is likely to be a reduction in their capacity to function effectively.

The downsizing, re-engineering and increased competitiveness that characterised corporate life in the UK during the 1980s and 1990s produced high levels of unproductive pressure in many working environments. People have found themselves being called upon to work too hard and to achieve too much, with too few resources in a context that was being transformed too rapidly. Even senior managers felt that they had no choice about working more than they wanted, and many reported that they no longer looked forward to work. About a quarter of those who replied to one survey said that they were always anxious, irritable and prone to disturbed sleep patterns (Charlesworth 1998). With some reports suggesting that over a quarter of Britain's full-timers work more than 48 hours a week, and that some 45 per cent of the workforce in the UK come home exhausted, the consequences of such developments for the quality of parenting may be serious (PAW 1995). The American sociologist Richard Sennett has written of how changes in the workplace, by corroding the qualities of trust, loyalty and mutual commitment, have left parents uncertain about how they can communicate these qualities to their children (Sennett 1998).

Many of the strategies being proposed by occupational psychologists to deal with the problems of stress-related illness and under-performance in the workplace are attempts to enhance people's emotional resilience so that they can make better choices for themselves, and deal more effectively with the emotional pressures they experience at home and in the workplace (Cooper and Williams 1994). Approaches include providing opportunities for individuals to reflect upon their experiences of work, and encouraging the development of group contexts in which emotional issues can be articulated and people can learn to become more open about the difficulties that they face. In this way they may come to recognise that others may be no better at coping than they are, and learn that it is okay to ask for help.

The wider context

Also contributing to the heightened level of emotional pressure and insecurity being experienced by individuals are a series of social changes, such as the fragmentation of family life, the weakening of community support structures, and the insecurity of employment patterns. These changes increase people's need for emotional literacy at the same time as they undermine the conditions for achieving it. In the book mentioned above, Richard Sennett describes how the changes introduced by the 'new capitalism' have made it more difficult for people to construct a coherent narrative of their own lives, giving them a sense of who they are and where they might be heading (Sennett 1998). This is a gap that needs addressing at many levels, through promoting the sort of collaborative and dialogic relationships that facilitate an understanding of the self in relation to others. It is by making such processes possible in the family, the workplace and on a wider social plane that one ensures people develop the skills necessary to maintain sensitive relationships with each other.

Parenting projects which have been set up as part of a community's efforts to regenerate itself, such as the Shankill Road Project in Belfast mentioned above, will tend to recognise the need for participants to develop an understanding of their personal histories in relation to what has happened in the community, and to build a sense of empowerment in social relationships. Such projects fill a gap that has been created by the decline in levels of participation within political parties and community institutions. They recognise too that much of the cynicism that has grown up in the attitude of the public to politicians reflects people's sense that they have been stripped of agency and responsibility, at the same time as they have been exposed to processes of rapid change.

The project of encouraging better parenting needs to be linked to processes that engage people as citizens in thinking about and influencing the forces that shape the framework around their lives. There need to be fora in which people can work together on overcoming those feelings of anger, anxiety and hopelessness that have the potential to block their own development. In this way, it might be possible to break the pattern of a passive electorate entertaining impossible expectations of politicians, then expressing anger and disgust when their idealised hopes are dashed. The more positive self-esteem can be supported at the political level, the more impact will be made by those working with parents and their families.

Feeling–thoughts

The underlying theme of this chapter is that the quality of parenting in our culture is damaged by processes that operate to disconnect individuals from their affective lives. Any increase in internal pressure – whether coming from their relational, group or organisational context – has a tendency to insulate people from their emotions. Rebuilding the connections requires the development of multiple secure contexts where people can work to establish new understandings of themselves and other people.

There is an underlying need to challenge the tendency to view feeling as being somehow antithetical to thinking, and to recognise the damage that such a split does to ourselves and our communities. There are cultures which would view our determined efforts to disconnect the two as being incomprehensible (Wikan 1990), and would argue that the enemy of rationality is not the expression of emotions, but the shallowness in the way emotions are experienced and expressed. A strategy to reconnect feeling to rationality aims not only to improve the quality of parenting in our culture, but also to create a healthier emotional environment, one that will support the development to maturity of all our children.

Notes
1. National Coalition Building Institute, PO Box 411, Leicester LE4 8ZY.
2. Conflict and Change, 2a Streatfield Ave., East Ham, London E6 2LA.

References

Antidote (1997), *Realising the Potential: Emotional Education for All.* Antidote, 5th Floor, 45 Beech Street, London EC2Y 8AD.

Antidote (1998), *The Fourth R: Emotional Education in the Curriculum.* Antidote, address as above.

Bentley, T. (1998) *Learning Beyond the Classroom: Education for a Changing World.* London: Routledge/Demos.

Bowlby, J. (1973) *Attachment and Loss,* vol. 2. 369. New York: Separation, Basic Books.

Bowlby, J. (1988) *A Secure Base.* Harmondsworth: Penguin.

Brown, G. W. (1982), 'Early loss and depression', in Parkes, C. M., Stevenson-Hinde, J. (eds) *The Place of Attachment in Human Behaviour.* London: Tavistock.

Charlesworth, K. (1998) *Are Managers Under Stress?,* London: The Institute of Management (2 Savoy Court, Strand, London WC2R OEZ).

Cooper, C. and Williams, S. (1994) *Creating Healthy Work Organisations.* London: Wiley.

Fonagy, P., Steele, M., Steele, H., Higgitt, A., Leigh, T., Kennedy, R., Mattoon, G., Target, M. (1995) 'The predictive validity of mary main's adult attachment interview: A psychoanalytic and developmental perspective on the transgenerational transmission of attachment and borderline states', in Goldbeg, S., Muir, R., Kerr, J. (eds), *Attachment Theory: Social, developmental and clincal perspectives,* 237–78. Hillsdale, NJ: Analytic Press.

Fonagy, P. (1998) 'An attachment theory approach to treatment of the difficult patient', *Bulletin of the Meninger Clinic* **62**(2) 147–69.

Fraiberg, S. (1985) 'Ghosts in the nursery: a psychoanalytic approach to the problems of impaired infant-mother relationships', in *Selected Writings of Selma Fraiberg.* Ohio: Ohio State University Press.

Hinde, C. and Schwarz, J. (1994) 'Anxious romantic attachment in adult relationships', in Sperling, M., Berman, W. *Attachment in Adults,* New York: Guilford Press.

Holmes, J. (1993) *John Bowlby and Attachment Theory.* London: Routledge.

Mahler, M., Pine, F., Bergman, A. (1975) *The Psychological Birth of the Infant.* New York: Basic Books.

Main, M., Hesse, E. (1990) 'Parents' unresolved traumatic experiences are related to infant disorganized attachment status', in Greenberg, M. T., Cicchetti, D., Cummings E. M. *Attachment in the Pre-school Years.* Chicago: University of Chicago Press.

Main, M., Kaplan, N., Cassidy, J. (1985) 'Security in infancy, childhood and adulthood: a move to the level of representation', in Bretherton, I. and Waters, E. (eds) Growing Point of Attachment Theory and Research, *Monographs of the Society for Research in Child Development,* 50 (1–2, Serial No. 209), 66–104.

Marris, P. (1996) *The Politics of Uncertainty: Attachment in Private and Public Life.* London: Routledge.

Marrone, M. (1998) *Attachment and Interaction.* London and Bristol, Pennsylvania: Jessica Kingsley Publishers.

Mosley, J. (1996) *Quality Circle Time in The Primary Classroom.* Cambridge: LDA.

Murray, L., Kemton, C., Wolgar, M., Hooper, R. (1993) 'Depressed mothers' speech to their infants and its relation to infant gender and cognitive development', *Journal of Child Psychology and Psychiatry* **34**, 1083–1101.

PAW (Parents At Work) (1995) *Balancing Our Lives*, Annual Review 1994/5. Parents At Work, Fifth Floor, 45 Beech Street, Barbican, London EC2Y 8AD.

Perry, B. D. (1995) 'Childhood trauma: the neurobiology of adaptation and use-dependent development of the brain: how states become traits', *Infant Mental Health Journal* **16** 271–91.

Pound, A. (1990) 'The development of attachment in adult life – the NEWPIN experiment', *British Journal of Psychotherapy* **7**(1) Autumn, 77–85

Radke-Yarrow, M. (1991) 'Attachment patterns in children of depressed mothers', in Parkes, C. M., Stevenson-Hinde, J., Marris, P. (eds) *Attachment Across the Life Cycle.* London and New York: Tavistock.

Sennett, R. (1998) *The Corrosion of Character.* New York: Norton.

Simpson, J. A. and Rhodes, W. S. (1994) 'Stress and secure base relationships in adulthood', in Bartholomew, K. and Perlman, D. *Attachment Processes in Adulthood.* London and Bristol, Pennsylvania: Jessica Kingsley Publishers.

Sroufe, L. A. (1990) 'An organisational perspective on the self', in Cicchetti, D., Beeghly, M., (eds). *The Self in Transition: Infancy to Childhood.* Chicago: University of Chicago Press.

Steele, H. and Steele, M. (1994) 'Intergenerational Patterns of Attachment', in Bartholomew, K. and Perlman, D., *Advances in Personal Relationships*, vol. 5 *Attachment Processes in Adulthood.* London and Bristol, Pennsylvania: Jessica Kingsley Publishers.

Steele, H., Steele, M., Fonagy, P. (1996) 'Associations among attachment classifications of mothers, fathers and their infants: evidence for a relationship-specific perspective', *Child Development* **67**, 541–55.

Stern, D. (1985) *The Interpersonal World of the Infant.* New York: Basic Books.

Stern, D. (1995) *The Motherhood Constellation*, New York: Basic Books.

Thacker, J., Stoate, P., Feest, G. (1992) *Group Work Skills: Using Group Work in the Primary Classroom.* Exeter: Southgate.

Van Ijzendoorn, M. H., Juffer, F., Duyvesteyn, M. G. C. (1995) 'Breaking the intergenerational cycle of insecure attachment', *Journal of Child Psychology and Psychiatry*, **36**(2) 225–47.

White, M. (1992) *Self-Esteem – Its Meaning and Value in Schools.* Cambridge: Daniels Publishing.

Wikan, V. (1990) *Managing Turbulent Lives, A Balinese Formula for Living.* Chicago: University of Chicago Press.

Winnicott, D. W. (1967) 'Mirror-role of the mother and family in child development', in Lomas, P. (ed.) *The Predicament of the Family: A psycho-analytical symposium.* London: Hogarth.

SECTION THREE:

Relating principles to practice

Chapter 8

Supporting parents through parenting programmes

Bopinder Samra

Introduction

This chapter gives an account of support that was offered to parents and carers of young children through parenting skills programmes and workshops within an urban, inner city area, the London Borough of Newham in the East End of London. Due to the nature of funding which predominantly came through the City Challenge project the programmes were delivered in the Stratford end of Newham as this fell within the City Challenge boundaries. Also explored in the chapter is the background to Newham, details of the programme model, delivery and the benefits reaped by participants involved in the programmes/workshops.

The author has been involved in running a number of the parenting skills programmes both in English and other community languages in Newham as described in this chapter and is currently devising programmes for parents of young adolescents.

Background

London Borough of Newham is an inner London borough which is characterised by its cultural diversity. There are about 105 different languages spoken by the residents of Newham.

Newham is also acknowledged to be one of the most deprived areas in the country, with high levels of unemployment, poverty, a transitional population and significant levels of social deprivation and underachievement.

It is now a recognised fact both nationally and internationally (OECD 1997) by education based and research organisations that involving parents in education generally, and in the progress of their children specifically, can be a significant factor in raising educational achievement among children. It is also acknowledged that raising of parental achievement is necessary if the aims of economic regeneration are to be met and the underlying obstacles of poverty, poor housing, health and family break-up are to be overcome.

Newham has a long history of encouraging parental involvement in education and was the first authority to have parent representatives on the Education Committee, now contained in the 1998 Education Act. In 1992 the Education Committee adopted a policy on *'Parents as Partners in Education'*. The policy was the result of a wide-ranging consultation exercise involving parents, schools and other parent workers working within education.

Since the development of the policy much has been done to develop and encourage parental involvement in Newham schools (Wolfendale 1996a). Many of the initiatives fall within the three main areas identified within the policy:

- raising levels of achievement by young people;
- raising levels of parents' personal achievement and involvement.
- promoting community education and equal opportunities;

The most recent development was the launch of the **Learning Community Strategy** in January 1997 which mainly focuses on raising educational achievement of the whole community. The strategy aims to develop a learning community, which values education for children, young people, adults and as a lifelong process for all.

The main objectives to be met through the strategy are to:

- raise expectations among young people and adults;
- secure active support for strategies designed to raise levels of achievement of children, young people and adults;
- maximise parental and wider community involvement in young people's education;
- increase motivation of and participation by children in the education and learning process;
- build a partnership to promote the learning community strategy.

It has been possible to develop parental involvement initiatives in the LEA schools over the years through the availability of funding through the Adult Literacy and Basic Skills Unit (ALBSU), Section 11, Urban Aid, London Dockland Development Corporation (LDDC), Grants for Education, Support and Training 19 and 20 (GEST 19, GEST 20), City Challenge and the Education Department's Main Grants programme.

The recent changes in the funding of the post 16 education have put increasing pressures on the local authority. These have limited LEAs being able to respond to the learning needs of parents other than in preparation for work or to a limited extent in their roles as parents. The extent to which parents have educational opportunities themselves is important for several reasons:

- the home learning atmosphere is often linked to parents' personal experience of learning, either as a child or as an adult;
- the level of parental achievement is linked to the economic attainment of the family;
- the level of children's attainment is linked to both the home learning atmosphere, parents' personal experience and the family's level of economic well-being.

Newham LEA has and still is pioneering a considerable amount of work in the field of involving parents in supporting their children's learning, but little was available around parenting skills programmes. Therefore, in 1995 a further bid was made to extend the already successful *City Challenge – Action for Achievement* project to incorporate support and training on parenting skills for parents and carers, which the rest of this chapter focuses on.

Extension project – parenting programmes

In June 1995, I was appointed to lead the extension project. Having worked closely with parents in Newham schools for 13 years in the capacity of an Outreach/Science teacher, Raising Achievement Coordinator and a Deputy Head of House, and also having interacted with the local community during this time, I was aware of the parenting issues that needed addressing for both the British and the ethnic minority parents. Being able to speak four of the local community languages and through my links having easy access to speakers of other community languages, I welcomed this opportunity to organise, devise and run parenting programmes not only in English but also in other community languages.

The extension project aimed to provide a programme for parents to raise their awareness of the personal, social, psychological, emotional, developmental and educational needs of young children, with emphasis on increasing parental confidence and self-esteem.

Keeping the extension project's aim in mind some initial time was spent researching the availability of parenting programmes, both locally and nationally, setting up initial meetings with schools, nurseries, health visiting team, local community centres and voluntary organisations in the City Challenge area, liaising with crèche workers and the borough's under 8's inspection and registration team, visiting local play groups and publicising the programme.

In September 1995, the first set of pilot programmes was launched at three primary schools and one nursery school in the City Challenge area in Stratford. Initially programmes like *Parent Link* and *Caring Start* that were already available on the market were used as pilots to see if they met the needs and demands of Newham parents. Family Service Unit (FSU) of Barking and Dagenham was also contacted for the initial delivery as the coordinator had previously run some programmes in Newham.

- **Parent Link** (The Parent Network) aims to provide support and education to make the day-to-day ups and downs of family life as easy and rewarding as possible.
- **Caring Start** (High/Scope) aims to enhance the child's self-esteem, confidence, self-control and self discipline through activities and support from adults who interact with the child to promote physical, intellectual and social development.

All three programmes had elements in them which enhanced parental confidence and self-esteem and focused on the needs and wants of young children, but it was felt there still was a need to create programmes that were tailored to the needs of Newham's diverse community. While the courses relevant to Newham's community were being developed, the demand for parenting programmes was growing at a great speed. Parents, grandparents and carers from various ethnic communities were also requesting similar programmes to be run in their own community languages. These requests enabled us to pilot the courses devised for Newham's parents and modify each one so that it identified with the particular community that we were trying to reach.

Participants

To date, 550 parents/carers have participated in the programme/ workshops and participants represented most of Newham's major ethnic minority communities. The key workers (City Challenge co-ordinator and myself) being able to speak four of the local community languages and having had vast experience of working with ethnic minority groups, hence also being able to access and train workers from other minority groups made it possible to deliver the programmes in Urdu, Hindi, Punjabi, Bengali and Somali. Male carers, although far fewer in number than female carers, also accessed the programme. The programme has also attracted parents and carers with special needs (for example dyslexic, blind and partially deaf). (See Table 8.1.)

Links with other agencies

The extension project has collaborated successfully with a range of voluntary and statutory organisations in Newham in the delivery of the programmes. Good working links have been developed with other agencies like Social Services, Early Years Unit, Newham Community Health Service Trust, Community Education Service, Stratford Development Partnership, Community Centres, Children Centres, Advice Arcade, Play Groups and Mother and Toddler Groups to enhance, access and promote the project.

Table 8.1

	Number of *programmes/ workshops and language of delivery	Parents/carers attending in year
Year 1 April 95–March 96	14 programmes in English 1 programme in Urdu 1 programme in Punjabi	136
Year 2 April 96–March 97	16 programmes in English 2 programmes in Somali 1 programme in Bengali 5 workshops in English	203
Year 3 April 97–March 98	10 programmes in English 27 workshops in English	211

* Programmes were of five to six weeks' duration
Workshops were of two to four week duration.

Programme model

The project developed a model using a programme of five or six weeks duration, which ran parallel with the school term time, and was accompanied by a crèche. Such a model not only enabled parents to attend the parenting skills programme in peace, but made them feel valued as individuals and gave them a sense of satisfaction, as they saw it as time out for themselves without any disturbance or bother from the children.

Comments made by parents on time out for themselves:

'The programme was really enjoyable. It was nice to have an afternoon to myself, talking and listening to other parents in similar circumstances.'

'I have not been in contact with women of my age group in a long time. This programme gave me the opportunity to do so and to be away from the kids.'

'It gave me a nice break from my three-and-a-half-year-old. I got to meet other women living in my area and talked about how we each cope with our children and our feelings.'

'It gave us an opportunity to meet other people, share experiences and relax.'

'It was very helpful as it gave us time to talk together about our own positive qualities and that of our children.'

Evaluation

All the parenting programmes were evaluated on a weekly basis and after a period of about six to eight weeks after completion of the programme by running a post-programme *Focus Group* of the participating parents. The comments made by the parents on the evaluation sheets indicate that they not only enjoyed the programmes but also benefited from them.

Comments made by parents who have been on the programmes

'This course has given me a real boost, I feel more positive about myself and about how I'm bringing up the children.'

'It gives me a sense that I'm not fighting and losing the battle on my own, that there are others in the same situation.'

'I have learned about the mixed messages we give our children.'

'I try and keep calm and think before reacting. I try and remember to praise good behaviour and try to ignore bad behaviour.'

'My husband made sure he reminded me about the parent classes today because he is also learning from my notes and what I share with him.'

'I was able to share experiences and ideas, it gave me some time away from the children and to think about new ideas.'

'To know that I'm not alone, other parents face the same problems.'

'It helped me realise that each child is unique and has different needs.'

'It was very informative – A good approach to looking at alternative ways of dealing with children and their behaviour as well as our own.'

'The programme is very good, especially for mothers. I congratulate the authority that introduced it.'

'It tackles all those well-known problems like surviving a trip to the supermarket, eating problems, temper tantrums and more. '

'Planning together and good delegation helps both the children and myself.'

'I have learnt to keep calm, count to ten and sit down and talk to my children.'

'The programme makes you realise that children are like us and have feelings and we have to respect them.'

The programmes have not only made parents/carers more informed about the development of their children and affected the way they act as parents/carers but also helped them to build up their confidence, raise their self-esteem, develop further in training, education, work and in their contribution to community. For example:

- One parent who participated in the programme that was offered in a community language now helps in a nursery class.
- Another who previously required substantial help and support from school now works as a dinner lady, has taken on playground duties and has also performed locally in a production on parenting.

The comments made by parents have been analysed by Professor Sheila Wolfendale, who was appointed as an external evaluator for the project. In her evaluation reports for 1996–8 she states:

The set of returned sheets provide a source of rich data. The verbatim responses provide eloquent and enduring testimony to the overwhelmingly positive effects of course attendance on:

- participant's attitudes to themselves as parents (increased self-esteem and confidence)
- their expressed effectiveness as 'managers' of their children.

What also comes across in reading the evaluation sheets is the nature of the progression towards increasing self-confidence, reappraisal of methods of child rearing and behaviour management. Course attendance, meetings and sharing common childrearing issues has been a catalyst to personal growth. The use of feedback sheets is thus affirmed as a means of formative evaluation. Parents' comments provide a lasting and direct record of their views.

In her evaluation report for 1997 Sheila Wolfendale groups verbatim comments under a number of themes, for example:

- General value for parents in their role of parent
  'I can now be more confident with my children, and not feel that I am failing them.'
- Value in their role as behaviour manager
  'I feel that I can manage my children better.'
  'How I can listen to my child.'
- Specific skill gains
  'I have learned communication skills.'
- Learning practical strategies
  'Reduce stress levels'.
- Confirmation that they are not alone, in having parental anxieties and lack of confidence.
  'A lot of us seem to have the same problems as parents.'
- Having greater understanding of the parental role
  'Being given a wider view of things.'
- General gains in confidence in being a parent
  'I feel that I am generally more positive now to my children.'

- Having realistic expectations
'Everyone handles situations differently, and different environments make different kinds of children.'

See Chapter 4 by Sheila Wolfendale for further explanation and comment.

From a methodological standpoint the chosen instruments for evaluation retrospectively appear to have been appropriate and adequate for the task. They enabled process as well as outcome data to be obtained. The instruments seem robust and fit the purpose. Given the restricted amount of time, they have proved an efficient method of data collection and recording. The number of returns has been valuable and solid enough to provide plenty of information.

Key successes and spin-offs

Case Study A

Just when the attendance of parents/carers at the parenting programmes and other parental initiatives in schools and nurseries was flourishing, Theatre Venture – an East London Arts Company, was looking to involve the local community in a theatre production. The production coordinator heard of the parents' groups coming into schools through the LEA's City Challenge Action for Achievement project. He approached the project coordinator in order to bring together a group of parents, who were already involved in schools, to work on a theatre production.

The parents who had just finished attending the six-week parenting skills programme and whose confidence had grown were keen to move on to something new. They saw this as an opportunity to achieve something for themselves. The majority of the parents who became involved with the theatre production were single mothers. As a result of their work with Theatre Venture the parents put on a production around parenting. This contained some very good and moving songs on parenting which proved to be very popular not only in the production but also at a seminar which was organised in Newham through the project. Since then the parents' group have received invitations both locally and nationally to make their presentations. This certainly is rewarding for the parents and their children. Newham is certainly proud of the parents' achievements and also of the collaborated work with other agencies that can move people on.

Two songs on parenting that proved to be very popular are reproduced here with the kind permission of the parents.

The first song, *Domestic Engineer*, was sung by Vanessa Huby, Sally Joshi, Zena Pitcher, Beverly Slingo, Joanne Tonner and Lynn Wakefield.

Domestic Engineer

Cooking and cleaning and ironing and washing up
And tidying, taking to school – and picking up
Keeping the kids occupied, having their friends around to play
A twenty-four hour job every day
Entertainer, Cook and Cleaner and I'm here – The Domestic
   Engineer.

Shopping and dressing and mending and sorting out
Their puzzles and squabbles 'Don't make me have to shout.'
Praising, encouraging, giving them time when I'm feeling stressed
Staying awake when I just want to rest
A Referee and a Counsellor – I'm here The Domestic Engineer
                                        The Domestic Engineer.

I take them here – I take them there
To Judo and Swimming – 'I take them everywhere.'
I show them how to dress – 'No you *can't* wear that!'
And how to share – 'Oy! Give that back!'

A diplomat – A fashion consultant
I do it for love – not for a company car
Or twenty thousand pounds a year
A Domestic Engineer
A Domestic Engineer.

Keeping them happy while I change the baby's nappy
Helping with their homework – helping them to read and write
Teaching them road signs and how to ride a bike
Putting cream on their eczema every night
A nurse and a teacher and I'm here – 'the Domestic Engineer
                                        The Domestic Engineer.

I sacrifice my *Home and Away* so that they can watch the
   Simpsons
I might paint a wall or unblock the sink while I watch them play.

A plumber – A decorator
I do it for love – not for a company car
Or twenty thousand pounds a year
A Domestic Engineer A Domestic Engineer
A Domestic Engineer.

Entertainer, Cook and Cleaner, Referee and Counsellor
Diplomat, Fashion Consultant
Teacher, Nurse
Plumber and Decorator – but I don't get no pay
A twenty-four hour job every day
I'm always here

The Domestic Engineer – No – Not *just* a house wife
The Domestic Engineer – Not *just* a mother
The Domestic Engineer.

The second song, *No time for me*, was sung by Vanessa Huby.

No time for me
Being a parent, what does it mean?
At first I was excited, now I'm not so keen
I don't think I really had a clue
And now she's growing up, what am I going to do?

At first she was a baby – Aah...
That wasn't so bad
But she's just turned six and she's up to her tricks
And I think I'm going MAD!

Do this, Do that, that's all I seem to say
But will she ever listen? I'm waiting for the day!
I'm your mum – I've got no time to explain
Just do as you're told – I won't tell you again!

Maybe I should sit her down
Try to tell her what I mean
But when I look around I think I'm gonna drown
In all the washing and the things I've got to clean.

What is my life? – What does it mean? – No time for me (*repeat*)

Oh there's so much more to being a mum
Add it all up – it'll be a big sum
Everyone says, 'You're doing a job.'
But I don't know what I'm doing – I think I'm going to sob.

I'm on my own, haven't even got a phone
I'd try to get away if I could get a loan
Been moaning all day – I'll blame it on the hormones
I'm just too tired to find a rhyme for hormones (*Yawn*)

What is my life? – What does it mean? – No time for me (*repeat*)

The day is nearly done
Her story's been read
Do you know what she said as I tucked her into bed
'You all right mum?' and I kissed her on the head

It's not so bad being a mum
I have my ups and downs but doesn't everyone
And I can't deny that she made me smile
The things she says – make it all worth while.

Case study: B

A seminar to celebrate the *European Year of Lifelong Learning* was held in Newham in 1997. The seminar aimed to further develop and enhance provisions for families. The role of families as the foundations for lifelong learning was the theme of the seminar, which attracted a variety of both local and national participants, among them parents, education workers, teachers, school governors, health visitors, social workers, voluntary sector workers and others working with families.

Newham's Learning Community Strategy which aims to improve the climate of learning in Newham schools and encourage a commitment to education in the wider community was also launched on the day. The seminar offered delegates an opportunity to listen to a panel of speakers and attend workshops. The speeches and workshops had an equal representation from both professionals and parents.

Victoria Williams and Onikepe Ijete, both from ethnic minority backgrounds, spoke about the benefits they had received having attended the Parenting Skills Programme.

Victoria informed delegates how the Parenting Skills Programme had helped her at the time when she was experiencing great difficulties in the stages of parenting.

> 'The programme itself educated me as a mother, and I think with the help, encouragement and friendliness of my programme leaders, it has given me a zeal and hunger for going onto further education, and study an in-depth advanced course, for children with special needs, based on curiosity for further knowledge'.

Onikepe, a medical doctor who also attended the Parenting Skills Programme, shared with conference delegates how prior to attending the programme she thought that once a child was fed, cleaned and protected from physical harm she had met the needs of her child. But now, after attending the programme, she realised that her child had many other needs, which were not being met as she had been unaware of them.

> 'I learnt from the course that in order to create in my daughter confidence and good self-esteem, I needed to start with myself. After all, a child who is confident and has good self-esteem grows up to become a confident adult with a good self-image. I learnt to see my daughter not just as a child, but as a human being with needs like me – an adult – perhaps even more so considering that the world must seem a strange and bewildering place to a child, who is just learning to cope with everyday things which we as adults take for granted. I learnt that my daughter misbehaved at times not just because she wanted to be naughty but because she wanted attention. I learnt how

to give her positive attention instead of the instinctive negative one, for example, shouting, screaming, scolding or criticising. I also learnt to listen to her and to talk with her and not at her, I learnt the importance of spending quality time with her.

'I was also able to re-evaluate my relationship with adults. It occurred to me that, for instance, if a person needs someone to listen to him or her, then this need would not just disappear just because that person was now an adult. Perhaps there were a lot of people out there needing to be noticed, needing to be made to feel important, and needing to be listened to. I decided to try it out on people I already knew and people I came across in the course of my daily activities. It worked! Now I have a lot more friends – when you make people feel good they want to be around you.

'I feel this is a programme that every parent needs to be on. When you really think about it, if one wanted to learn how to drive one would need driving lessons. Why shouldn't the same apply to parenting?'

Other key successes

Apart from the active involvement of the parents in an inter-agency seminar where they made speeches, lead workshops and sang songs produced by them in collaboration with Theatre Venture staff, other key successes have been:

- More and more parents wanting to go on to further education, training and employment.
- Parents becoming involved in their children's nurseries and schools.
- Parents not feeling inhibited coming on to school premises.
- Parents for whom the courses were held in Urdu, Punjabi, Bengali, and Somali are making enquiries for further education and training, and some have succeeded in finding employment in spite of having limited command of spoken and written English.
- Monies from other sources outside the borough coming into the borough.
- The piloting of the Bengali and Somali *Caring Start* parenting programmes (High/Scope) in Newham which are now on the national and international market.
- The programmes/workshops attracting fathers and parents with special needs.
- Local courts directing parents to attend these programmes before being given access to their children.
- Two programmes piloted for parents of young adolescents.
- Participants reporting back on benefits gained from having attended the programmes/workshops and requesting extension courses.
- Parents becoming more open about the help and support needed by them.

Conclusion

The project has been successful in running the now established parenting programmes and making parents/carers more informed about children's social and educational development. The demand and need for parenting skills programmes and support for parents/carers in Newham are on the increase. This is supported by the number of enquiries made about the availability of the programmes by parents, health services, social services, child and family consultation service, secondary schools, children's centres and community groups.

Some of the secondary schools are also very keen to set up programmes for parents of young teenagers. As mentioned earlier, Newham has already piloted two programmes for parents of young adolescents and is in the process of making arrangements for other such programmes to be run in secondary schools. The funding for these is being met through the LEA's *Learning Community Budget.* A recent request made by an ethnic minority group to run the programme for young Punjabi mothers is being looked into. Newham's Community Education Service in partnership with the Community group is hoping to fund this initiative. Newham's Community Education Service has also been supportive in funding such initiatives in the schools which fell outside the City Challenge area but requested similar programmes be run on their premises.

Newham has a rapidly expanding population of under 5's that is projected to continue to increase and is a diverse community with diverse needs. The parents and carers who participated in the parenting programmes welcomed the support and reported to have benefited immensely from them, therefore it is crucial to continue with such support for other parents and carers.

Titus Alexander (1977) mentions in his seminar report *Empowering Parents* that:

> 'Families are the most important place of learning in the world.' If we really understand what this means, we will revolutionise the way in which we organise education, public services and the economy. Instead of treating family life as a cost, we would treat it as our most important investment for the future. For better or worse, parents are the most influential educators in most people's lives. Yet we spend very little time or money supporting parents. Instead parents are blamed when things go wrong and huge amounts of money are spent on coping with the consequences of families living under stress. (*Empowering Parents*, p.1 para1)

Focusing on what Titus Alexander says, in Newham we are trying our best to support families within the limited budget constraints. Parenting education and support is now included in our Early Years Development Plan and the delivery and funding availability for the future is being looked into.

Newham used a model that worked and attracted parents, as mostly schools and nurseries were used as venues and parenting programmes were incorporated within the framework of other parental involvement initiatives developed in schools. This model of working is supported by Pugh and her colleagues: 'Parent workshops are seen by some as making an important contribution to the bridge linking home to school' (Pugh *et al.* 1994, p.78). They further refer to Hinton (1987) who concludes from her report on parent workshops attached to primary and nursery schools that:

> By developing parents' ability to enlist the co-operation of their children we are not only alleviating parents' problems, and perhaps averting later ones, but laying the foundation-stone for effective parental involvement in children's education. Some will argue that parent education in the field of behaviour management is not the responsibility or the concern of schools. However, this study illustrates how a multi-professional approach incorporating the interest and support of teachers can enhance the effectiveness of an intervention for the benefit of the child in school as well as at home. (Pugh *et al.* 1994, p.78).

Being a parent/carer is one of the most demanding jobs in the world and it is unpaid. As parents/carers one is not only trying to meet the basic needs of children, like feeding them, getting them to school and keeping them clean, but also being their teachers, nurses, doctors, counsellors, instructors, chauffeurs, repair persons, advocates, role models. Parents/carers do their best in bringing up children but often find the task exhausting and leaving themselves wondering 'are they doing what is right for their children'. Sometimes just that reassurance from other parents, either through parenting programmes or support groups, gives parents the confidence to deal with everyday situations and so feel less stressed.

In Newham, having run parenting programmes for a diverse community which included a number of ethnic minority groups, I generally found that most parents, regardless of their background, had a lot of issues and concerns that were common regarding the upbringing of children. Though it cannot be denied that there are some issues that are very specific to a particular ethnic group which obviously needed to be, and were, addressed differently, on the whole all parents welcomed and valued the support they received through the programmes. They reported that they were generally getting more and more interested in their child as a whole person and were also starting to value themselves and the job that they were doing as parents.

References

Alexander, T. (1997) *Empowering Parents: families as the foundation of a learning society, 1.* London: National Children's Bureau.

Caring Start, High/Scope, The High/Scope Institute UK, 190–192 Maple Road, London SE20 8HT.

Hinton, S. (1987) 'A study of behaviour management workshops for parents of nursery school children'. Unpublished thesis, Institute of Education, University of London.

OECD (1997) *Parents as Partners in Schooling.* Paris: Organisation for Economic Co-operation and Development, Centre for Educational Research and Innovation.

Parent Link, *The Parent Network*, 44–46 Caversham Road, London NW5 2DS.

Pugh, G., De'Ath, E., Smith, C. (1994) *Confident Parents, Confident Children*, 78. London: National Children's Bureau.

Wolfendale, S. (1996a) 'The contribution of parents to children's achievement in school: policy and practice in the London Borough of Newham', Chapter 8 in Basiani, J. and Wolfendale, S. (eds) *Home-School Work in Britain, Review, Reflection and Development.* London: David Fulton Publishers.

Wolfendale, S. (1996b) *City Challenge – Action for Achievement Evaluation of Project A, London Borough of Newham*, 8–9. Department of Psychology, University of East London.

Wolfendale, S. (1997) *City Challenge – Action for Achievement Fourth Evaluation Report*, 16. Department of Psychology, University of East London.

Chapter 9

Support for parents at significant times of transition

Sonya Hinton

Introduction

In Surrey the Educational Psychology Service has developed a range of interventions to support parents as particular needs became apparent. This has happened in what, at first, seemed a rather haphazard way. However on reflection the accumulated strategies have a coherence, albeit with gaps still to be filled, focusing on significant transitions in the parent–child life cycle. It is the parents themselves who highlight for professionals the points on the journey of parenting where information and support is most needed. The purpose of this chapter is to share with others practices that have proved useful in supporting parents at those points in the life cycle when a significant number of parents have sought our help. The packages have been developed in order to make them available to a wider audience since it has become increasingly apparent that the parents who actively seek our help represent but the tip of the iceberg. They are those for whom the various experiences cause problems while many more are anxious or curious and would welcome more information, ideas and opportunities to reflect on their handling of particular transitions.

Educational psychologists have a unique opportunity to work at the interface between those parents who experience significant difficulties in raising their children and the vast majority who weather the inevitable ups and downs of parenting, snatching what support they can from family and friends, magazine articles and television programmes. Working in schools educational psychologists are very conscious not only that parents want help when things go wrong but that they actively seek information and the opportunity to talk about approaching changes and stages. It is for all parents that these interventions have been developed, as affirmation for the many and as support for the few who are in difficulties.

White and Woollett (1992) maintain that parenthood calls for constant adjustments and remains a transitional state throughout children's lives. It is by its very nature an ever changing challenge, demanding constant adaptation to the changing needs of the developing child. There are times of significant transition when the need to adapt and change the style of parenting increases. For some parents transitions are particularly challenging and can be daunting in prospect and hard to handle in practice. It is at these times that families are more at risk of breakdown and may need the help of expensive, specialist support services. It is at these transitions too that we are both most vulnerable and most open to modifying our behaviour and attitudes. There are therefore strong educational, as well as humanitarian and financial arguments, for offering parents the opportunity to reappraise their approach to parenting at predictable times of change.

Family life cycles

The stresses on parents are best understood in the context of family life cycles. There are many factors that influence the pattern of the family life cycle including ethnicity, culture, and socio-economic status. It is therefore difficult to describe a 'normal' cycle; nonetheless all families are subject to the exits and entrances of family members by birth, cohabitation and by death.

Figure 9.1 depicts a single adult life cycle of which half makes up the parenting phase. However each individual life cycle takes place within a broader context of the three or even four generation family. These interlocking life cycles have all simultaneously to adjust to shifting phases. Thus the arrival of a first baby to an adult couple not only precipitates them into the role of parents but their sisters and brothers to aunts and uncles and their parents to grandparents.

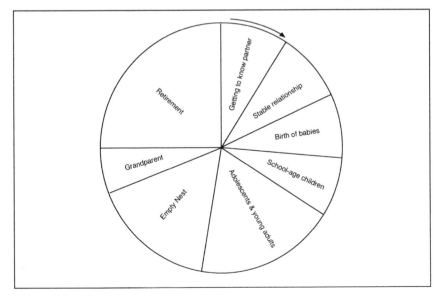

Figure 9.1

While the adult couple may have made a conscious decision to become parents there is no such assessing readiness for change nor decision-making for the rest of the family. The change in status is thrust upon them. Failure of any part of these interlocking systems to adapt to new roles and situations at transitions can increase the stress on other family members. In addition the way in which the previous generation has responded to transitions in their own life cycle has a significant effect on the next generation's coping strategies. An interesting recognition of the importance of this inter-generational influence is a 'grandparent class' held currently as part of the antenatal preparation courses run by the Royal Surrey County Hospital, South West Surrey Regional Health Authority.

Some significant transitions in the parenting life cycle such as the birth of the first baby, starting school and death of family members are encountered by all parents. There are other events, the birth of subsequent babies, moves of house, separation, divorce and the creation of new family units faced by a proportion of all parents. How parents manage these events and adapt their parenting to meet the needs of their children depends on a multiplicity of factors, such as parental personality, the child's disposition, their own experience in childhood and the social networks that are available to support them. Research in the field of parenting education is only just beginning to analyse these factors and investigate how they influence family resilience and parents' ability to make use of the range of available support services.

What is available to parents has only been documented fairly recently (notably by Smith (1996) in *Developing Parenting Programmes*). Research is also showing that what parents really want from parenting education is to learn from other parents and to raise their self-esteem. They hope to gain a range of strategies for handling children's difficult behaviour and that family relationships will improve as a result of attending courses.

In Surrey there is a recognition of the need to develop and evaluate as wide a range of services as possible, building on existing good practice. Increasingly collaboration between statutory and voluntary bodies is resulting in more comprehensive support for parents from which they can choose what suits them best. To further this collaboration one of the tasks of Surrey Education Department's newly created Parent Strategy Group is to catalogue all available resources within the county. In one area of Surrey a forum for all parenting education leaders has been set up under the auspices of the Health Promotion Unit to raise awareness of the range of opportunities available locally and to consider how to disseminate this information more widely to parents.

'If society is to do its best for children, changing social attitudes to parenting is a primary task' (Leach 1994, p.244). Offering support to all at the times of inevitable and universal transition when parents are most receptive to new ideas may open the way to normalising parent education in general and to overcoming the still prevalent view that parenting education is only for those with problems.

The initiatives described in this chapter have been developed by the Surrey Educational Psychology Service to offer information and support at some key points of transition in the parenting life cycle. There are six packages, two of which, 'The ABC of Behaviour' and 'Living with Teenagers' address transition in the *developmental* life cycle and four, 'Right from the Start', 'Getting Ready for School', 'Making the Move' and 'Preventing and Reducing Examination Stress' that address *educational* transitions. These packages adopt a range of approaches to providing parents with information and support from straightforward reading material to interactive group work. (See end of chapter References section for additional information relating to these packages.)

Helping with parenting in the early years

Forewarned, in the case of toddlers, is not automatically forearmed. This is a critical stage when so many parents run into difficulties. They survive but may lose confidence in their ability to parent effectively. The delightful baby sitting in the pushchair, whom all stopped to admire, may suddenly become a whirlwind, striding out and creating havoc. Tantrums in the supermarket produce glances from other people that embarrassed parents interpret as judgemental and critical. Starting school too may precipitate the expression of concerns by teachers about learning or behaviour that parents again feel reflect badly on their parenting. This toddler/young child stage is when many parents seek help because they want more specific guidance or because things seem to be going wrong.

The ABC of Behaviour
The Surrey Educational Psychology Service has developed a leader's manual for running parent workshops *ABC Workshops: Managing Children's Behaviour* (Hinton 1998). These are run in schools by psychologists and by health visitors, a method of delivery known to be acceptable to a significant proportion of parents according to a national study of parents and parenting problems undertaken by The Family Policy Studies Centre (Roberts *et al.* 1995). The study aimed 'to find out more about how parents seek help in facing and overcoming the everyday problems of bringing up children' and found that although the largest group of parents (26 per cent), turned first to their GP for help, the combined total of parents turning first to their health visitor or teacher was 39 per cent, indicating that support offered through these two channels is likely to be acceptable.

These parent workshops consist of a course of five or six weekly one hour sessions offered to parents of young children (2 to 7 year age group) usually in a nursery or school base. A crèche is provided in order to free parents to give their full attention to the group. In most cases these have been daytime sessions run to coincide with bringing or fetching children from school. The workshops are usually offered free to all parents wishing to participate, however some funding agencies require that places are kept for targeted families. Parents are recruited to the workshops, by poster, newsletter and by personal contact. The latter approach is the most effective in recruiting participants but carries with it the disadvantage, from the parents' point of view, of appearing to imply criticism of their parenting. Groups vary in size from 6 to 12 participants and consist predominantly of mothers, possibly because of the time of day at which the workshops are run. However evening sessions often present baby sitting problems and when offered as an extra session to enable partners to be involved has been poorly attended.

The group approach gives parents the opportunity to gain support from each other and to realise that they are not alone in finding their child challenging. They are reassured that their child is not abnormal and gain a better understanding of what they can reasonably expect from their child at this stage of development. They gain a grasp of the ABC framework to use as a way of approaching problem-solving when their usual repertoire of strategies runs out. Parents' success in applying these skills to problems of their own choice increases their confidence.

The course is structured around teaching parents the ABC problem-solving framework set out in the parent handbook, *The ABC of Behaviour – Troubleshooting for the Parents of Young Children* (Hinton 1994) which is provided at the beginning of the course. The parents use this framework, **A** for Antecedents, or triggers to the behaviour, **B** for a clear statement of the Behaviour and **C** the Consequences of the behaviour, to unpick challenging situations. They then use the framework and strategies discussed to arrive at a plan to address the child's particular problem. Group members support each other by suggesting new strategies and by encouraging each other to try new approaches. Each parent works out an intervention plan to put into practice at home and reports to the group on progress. Success with one difficulty boosts their confidence and has them rushing to tackle further concerns. Success also increases their confidence in their ability to use this model to resolve any future difficulties. The course leader is able to introduce a wide range of issues into the discussion according to the needs of the particular group.

Evaluation is always a thorny question. How do we reliably show that participants have gained useful skills which have a positive impact on children's behaviour when we are so often providing short-term intervention in complex systems?

A small evaluation study (Hinton 1988) showed a significant decrease in children's behaviour problems in the home following their parents' attendance at the workshops. While there was no significant measurable increase in parental self-esteem, qualitative responses indicated that parents had much greater confidence and enjoyment in their parenting role. Positive responses continue to feature in the feedback at the end of every workshop. For example here are some verbatim quotes from parent participants:

'I've given more thought to why the children behave as they do, realised it sometimes is reaction to my behaviour. I try very hard not to lose my temper and shout.'

'I'm calmer when dealing with children. Try to think ahead to stop the problem occurring.'

'I'm more patient, listen more.'

'I've learnt that reinforcing polite, positive, happy parenting is more rewarding than angry parenting.'

Perhaps the last word should be left with the nursery school head who remarked of the parents who had recently completed a workshop, 'Those parents come in now with their heads held high and their shoulders back'.

Right from the Start

An early transition for all families is the child's move into the reception class and statutory schooling. Although the majority of children will have had some pre-school experience this transition is seen by many parents as a milestone. While most children's first foray into the wider world is to child-minder, playgroup or nursery the start of 'big school' is still regarded as a marker, a rite of passage – a qualitative leap into full-time education. Registering with the school of your choice has to take place long before the child actually starts and it is often at this point that questions and concerns arise in parents' minds. 'Will she be ready, able to cope with so many other children, manage lunchtimes?' Coupled with these developmental concerns parents are also faced with the prospect of baseline assessment (Sainsbury 1998) and all that that may entail for their child. Government attention to educational standards, or the alleged lack of them and public debate about class size and teacher competence has increased parental concern. Add to this parents' own experience of the educational system and a situation exists in which parental anxieties are not easily assuaged, however reassuring the messages sent out by the authorities.

The motivation of parents at this time to do all they can to make the child's transition smooth and successful is high but they are not always sure what to do that will help. If they are to do the best they can by their children then parents need to be given some information about the challenges that face their children and an understanding of the skills needed to negotiate the transition successfully. Schools themselves provide much practical advice and statements of expectations as the new admissions procedures unfold but it was felt that earlier guidance to parents, during the year *before* entering the reception class, would help parents to understand how to support the development of their child's confidence and competencies to ensure a smoother transition to full-time education.

The Surrey Educational Psychology Service in conjunction with teachers and parents produced a booklet *Right from the Start: Helping Your Child in the Year Before School* (Hinton and Taylor 1993). The booklet grew out of concern for the parents' right to know about the constituent elements of the assessment that is carried out in school on all children shortly after admission. The child's teacher observes the child while completing a series of tasks in order to gain a picture of the child's skills against which future progress can be measured. It was felt that if educators considered certain skills to be important to a child's success in school then parents need to be given information about the experiences and activities that would promote children's development in these areas. The *Right from the Start* booklet sets out to answer some of the questions parents ask about how they can help their child get ready for school and what they can do at home to help. It makes suggestions for developing talking and listening, play, cooperation and independence as well as the more obviously educational issues such as getting ready for reading, writing, science and number work. Each page covers a single topic and is written in user-friendly language. The illustrations provide a focus for discussion with the child and often a colouring activity for an older sibling. The booklets can be bought from Surrey County Council (see References section for addresses) and are also available in many of Surrey's Libraries. Many Health Clinics also have these booklets available. Some schools offer the booklet to parents to buy while others have acquired funding from a variety of sources to enable them to distribute a free copy to each parent registering their child at school. Parental response has been enthusiastic. While the approach is common sense it provides an *aide-mémoire* for even the best-informed parents. One parent who was herself a nursery school teacher and whose third child was about to start school remarked that the booklet provided a prompt for her to give thought and attention to the process of transition.

Getting Ready for School

At the beginning of the term before entry to school 'Right from the Start' is followed by 'Getting Ready for School' (Hinton and Taylor 1994). This scheme consists of five activity packs and an accompanying parent information booklet to be used at home in the term before the transition to school. 'Getting Ready for School' is a carefully structured scheme originally developed in 1987 and updated and revised in 1994. It is based on well-established principles of motivation and learning including David Weikart's (1971) 'areas of cognitive development', a 'plan, do, review' approach to activities, in which children decide and plan how they will spend their time, carry out their plan and then are encouraged to reflect upon and report back on what they have done. Each pack is centred around a different cognitive area, size and shape, time, number, position and colour. Activities include suggestions for language, physical exploration and imaginative play around the theme of the pack. A story-book is included for the parent to share with the child. Also included are pencil skill activities, a turn taking board or card game and a taped story with accompanying talkabout picture, nursery rhyme sheets, and an action rhyme. A parent booklet with the packs provides some rationale for each individual activity as well as simple guidelines on carrying out the activities successfully. Much emphasis is put in the booklet on the importance of play, of the value of the child learning to make choices, of learning to cooperate and of taking turns. Above all it emphasises that the purpose of the packs is for the parent and child to have fun together and use the packs as a springboard to further shared activities. There is much informal evidence from parents' comments and children's enthusiasm to collect their packs that this is happening.

Schools vary in the ways they operate the scheme but the guidance suggests that the packs are introduced at a meeting held at school. Parents who fail to attend can be approached individually if staffing allows. The packs are then exchanged on a two-weekly basis. In some schools parent volunteers are used to operate the exchange system, checking in the packs and restocking them with the consumable materials. Many schools, however, find that the relationships built with the parents and children fully justify the use of the reception teacher's time to be present at the exchange session. Parents are enthusiastic about the scheme. Even those who say that they already do most of the suggested activities with their children see a benefit in the cooperative links it builds for them with the school. They appreciate the sense of familiarity and confidence that the children develop with their new school as well as enjoying the shared activities. For many children having the packs has become a part of the rite of passage to 'big school'.

Evaluation of this intervention at a quantitative level has proved difficult. It had been planned to compare results on the Surrey baseline screening test before and after introduction of the 'Getting Ready for School' packs. However changes to the screening materials themselves and a change of the age of admission to school at the time of the study invalidated any comparison of this kind. Evaluation of the impact of the materials in three schools in an area of high need met with disappointing response. Only 25 of the 80 questionnaires were returned by parents despite their enthusiastic participation in the scheme. Analysis of the parent questionnaires indicated that the areas in which parents thought using the packs had most impact were, in rank order:

- settling in to school;
- listening to stories;
- noticing detail in pictures;
- taking turns in games;
- learning nursery rhymes.

Eleven of the parents returning the questionnaires read more frequently to their children and twelve played more frequently with their children as a result of using the packs. Among those parents reporting that time reading and playing with their children had not increased because they were already spending time doing these activities still considered that their children had benefited from the scheme. One parent reported:

'The packs are very good, especially for parents that don't do much together. I have always spent a lot of time with my children, playing games, reading and just talking, but my son did feel he was getting big and doing important things for school, so he benefited in that way.'

Qualitative evaluation consistently yields very positive comments from both parents and teachers. Parental comments express both enthusiasm for the scheme:

'This pack is completely useful. Thank you for interesting pre-school programme.'

And provide rich information about the children:

'Another success. Nico has not stopped doing this pack. The tape has been great because he can listen with me and also do it on his own.'

'After helping her to understand the rhyme on the tape she was so excited and started singing correctly.'

One teacher commented:

'Excellent! It provides materials, opportunities and examples for families and begins at an appropriate time, to build relationships, shared experiences and expectations between home and school.'

Making the Move

Change is a significant feature of today's world, changes of school, of job and of partner will face many of our children. It is important therefore that parents and teachers provide children with an understanding of how change can be handled well with maximum gain and minimum stress to those involved.

Educationally the next significant transition for children and their parents is the move to secondary school. This is the first predictable transition that faces all children after they have developed the intellectual skills to reflect on the process. The majority of children of this age are able to internalise strategies for handling change in general while they are being helped with the immediate issue of successfully negotiating the transition to a particular secondary school. It is important therefore that teachers and parents capitalise on this opportunity to provide children with skills that will serve them for life. A great deal is being done by both primary and secondary schools to ease children's transition to secondary school, including an excellent workbook *Big School* (Maines and Robinson 1991) intended for use by primary schools. However very little material appears to be available to help parents support their children with the emotional aspects of transition.

A small-scale survey of parents, teachers and pupils in Years 6 and 7, the years before and after transfer, was carried out by the Surrey Educational Psychology Service to ascertain the nature of any concerns and the kind of information that might be helpful. This information was used to compile *Making the Move – Education for Change* (Hinton and Taylor, in press), a three part document with separate material for pupils, parents and teachers to be used at the beginning of Year 6 when the process of selecting a secondary school starts. The illustrated leaflet for pupils incorporates, as they had requested, comments by Year 7 pupils about what the move was like. The document for teachers explains the rationale for this intervention and suggests classroom activities. The parent booklet explains the rationale for highlighting this learning opportunity and provides some guidance on how they can help their child deal with the emotional as well as the practical aspects of leaving the familiar primary school to move into the unknown world of secondary school.

The teenage years

While the toddler stage often challenges parents, it is in the teenage years that parents need most help in reappraising their parenting role.

The secondary school years represent a long period of significant transition as the child grows into the young adult. At this stage, as with the younger age group, the majority of parents negotiate the phase without the need to access expensive support services. Today's thinking, however, is that 'All families need help to deal with the normal problems that occur from time to time. Easy access to help and information for parents at an early stage would prevent some of these problems developing into crises' (Report of the All Party Parliamentary Group on Parenting 1994, p.7).

Calls from parents to the telephone helpline Surrey Parentline, set up in 1994 peak during the teenage years. Calls from the parents of teenagers in the six-month period January to June 1998 accounted for 45.5 per cent of all calls.

At a conference in London in 1998, 'Supporting Parents of Teenagers: Policy and Practice', John Coleman of The Trust for the Study of Adolescence stated that 'it is apparent that the parents of teenagers lack useful information, both about normal adolescent development and about the sources of support should things go wrong. I will argue that we could develop a "route map" for parents, which would offer key elements of information at important milestones, such as the transfer to secondary school, and the move to post-16 provision. The creation and delivery of this "route map", would not be expensive but it could make a significant difference to parents and to teenagers.' There are clearly professed needs and an acknowledged dearth of material for the parents of teenagers. With the encouragement of The Trust for the Study of Adolescence funding is being sought for a pilot study to be carried out in one Surrey secondary school introducing a small booklet on adolescence to all parents as their children enter Year 7. The booklet outlines some of the normal physical, emotional and intellectual changes that occur during adolescence and suggests ways in which parents can adapt and maintain communication with their young person. It will also provide parents with information about sources of help and support in the local community.

Living with Teenagers

Surrey Educational Psychology Service offers a short parenting course to schools for all parents with pupils in Years 8 and 9. The material *Living with Teenagers – A Course Leader's Manual* (Hinton 1998) has been produced. The course is ideally offered as four workshop sessions with between 8 and 16 participants but where interest is high the initial session can be run as a large group with subsequent sessions being run as smaller workshops spread over time. The four sessions cover:

- Understanding the teenage years – How to live with your teenager with as little aggravation as possible.
- Being a good listener, learning how to listen well and choose the right words to get on better with your teenagers.

- What sort of a parent are you? – remembering what our parents did and deciding what we want to change or replicate.
- Dealing with conflict – thinking about how to deal with conflict, or better still, how to avoid it.

The methods used are predominantly oral with a small number of pencil and paper tasks. Minimal reading is required. The sessions have a 'circle time' structure in which the group agrees to ground rules of confidentiality and the 'fair shares' rule, ensuring equality of opportunity to contribute comments and problem share. Each session includes some leader input and structured pair and small group discussions.

Attendance figures and course evaluation suggest that parents both enjoy these workshops and acquire new perspectives and skills. Typical comments include:

'It gives you the chance to think about parenting without the pressure of your children and gives some insight into how others cope.'

'It is good to meet others who can share problems and their solutions – using other ideas for inspiration.'

'It's made me a lot calmer.'

'I think now I don't dictate.'

'Taught me how to phrase things better so as not to get into conflicts.'

'It's helped marriages too ... yes ... we've not had so many rows, in front of the boy anyway.'

A small sample of the teenagers whose parents attended the workshops reported that they saw their parents as 'less stressed' and 'better at hearing my point of view' after attending the workshops. There are plans to include the teenagers themselves in the final problem-solving session, 'Dealing with conflict'. The first half of the session would be run in separate groups and the second half in small mixed groups of parents and teenagers.

Reducing examination stress for parents and pupils

Another milestone for young people is when public examinations approach and the imminence of subject choices and career options looms. The importance of these examinations for the pupils can arouse a high level of anxiety not only in the young people themselves but also in their parents. In parents this feeling may be accompanied by feelings of frustration and powerlessness as they see their youngster wasting time, not working hard enough or conversely working too hard or becoming unduly stressed. All schools nowadays address the issues of study, revision skills and examination stress with pupils; however, not all schools do so with parents.

One scheme run in some Surrey schools has worked well in reducing the stress in families around the examination period. A number of other schools have adapted the model to fit in with the constraints of their particular situations. The blueprint for the scheme is that in addition to the normal curricular input on study skills the school invites parents and pupils to attend a workshop in the Autumn term during the lead up to 'mock' examinations.

This workshop is held in the evening and lasts about two hours. The first part of the evening is spent as a whole group and is led by the educational psychologist talking about the nature of stress and the tensions that can arise between parents and children in the lead up to examinations. The middle section of the evening is spent in separate groups, pupils working in tutor groups with teachers as leaders and the parents remaining with the psychologist. Pupils are provided with a handbook and revision planner which will act as a resource for them during the revision period and right through to the summer examinations. In their group pupils reflect on their own ways of handling pressure and are introduced to a range of strategies to reduce and deal with stress. Pupils are introduced to relaxation techniques which, given the short time available, have to be revisited either in PE lessons or as elective lunch hour sessions run by the school psychologist, school nurse or other interested adult. Relaxation audiotapes are also available. Parents explore, through group discussion, their own particular concerns as parents and discuss strategies for coping with stress. Parents and children then reunite for the final part of the evening. The common aim of parents and pupils is identified as being 'the best possible outcome for the pupils in the forthcoming examinations'. They then go on to work in separate small parent groups and pupil groups to consider two questions; pupils consider:

- What can parents do that would be helpful (in reducing stress and increasing chances of success); and
- What do parents do that is unhelpful?

Parents consider

- What could children do that would help? and
- What do children do that makes it difficult to help?'

Parents then join into groups with other people's children and both parents and pupils feed back and collate information about what is helpful and unhelpful. This is written down and collected in. The school later collates the 'helpful' suggestions for both pupils and parents into a leaflet for pupils to take home to share with their parents. The summing up is then carried out with the whole group by the head of year, or senior teacher, outlining the support that will be made available to students and parents during the examination period. It is at this point that parents and pupils can be told about revision sessions, relaxation training, extra lunchtime sporting opportunities, a parent telephone helpline or any other support the school is able to provide. The evening ends on an optimistic note predicting a successful outcome for all.

A leader's manual, 'Preventing and Reducing Examination Stress', is in preparation.

Conclusion

Some initiatives have been described that begin to address a few of the needs of families at points of significant transition. Validation comes not only in the satisfaction voiced by participating parents but in the gradual change in public perception of the rightful place of parenting support and education in society.

There is still much that could be done. As we listen to parents who participate in existing projects and to parents whom we meet in the course of our work but whose needs are currently not being met, further ideas for new support and education initiatives keep emerging. There is at last a mood and a will that acknowledges that:

> We have now no choice but to have massive investment in prevention while not neglecting some aspects, of course, of the much more expensive picking up of the pieces. (Professor Richard Whitfield in the Report of the All Party Parliamentary Group on Parenting, 1994, p.125)

References

Coleman, J. (1998) *Supporting Parents of Teenagers: Policy and Practice.* Proceedings of a day conference convened on 11 February 1998 by Parenting Education and Support Forum and The Trust for the Study of Adolescence.

Hinton, S. (1988) *A Study of Behaviour Management Workshops for Parents of Nursery School Children.* A Report submitted for an Associateship at the Institute of Education University of London.

Hinton, S. (1994) *The ABC of Behaviour – Troubleshooting for the Parents of Young Children.* Right from the Start Publications (SNS/CGS), Room 188, County Hall, Kingston upon Thames KT1 2DJ.

Hinton, S. (1997) *Living with Teenagers – A Course for Parents. Leader's Manual.* Right from the Start Publications (see address above).

Hinton, S. (1998) *ABC workshops: Managing Children's Behaviour: A Course Leader's Manual.* (see address above).

Hinton, S. and Taylor, A. (1994) *Getting Ready for School.* Right from the Start Publications (see address above).

Hinton, S. and Taylor, A. (in press) *Making the Move – Education for Change.* Right from the Start Publications (see address above).

Hinton, S., Taylor, A., Renny, J. (1993) *Right from the Start – Helping your Child in the Year Before School.* Right from the Start Publications (see address above).

Leach, P. (1994) *Children First.* London, Penguin.

Maines, B. and Robinson, G. (1991) *Big School.* Lucky Duck Publications, 34 Wellington Park, Clifton, Bristol BS8 2UW.

Report of the All Party Parliamentary Group on Parenting and International Year of the Family, UK Parliamentary Hearings (1994).

Roberts, C., Cronin, N., Dodd, T., Kelly, M. (1995) *The National Study of Parents and Parenting Problems.* The Family Policy Studies Centre, 231 Baker Stret, London NW1 6XE.

Sainsbury, M. (1998) Making Sense of Baseline Assessment. London: Hodder and Stoughton.

Smith, C. (1996) *Developing Parenting Programmes.* London: National Bureau Enterprises.

Weikart, D. (1971) *The Cognitively Oriented Curriculum.* High Scope: Ypsilanti.

White, D. and Woollett, A. (1992) *Families: A Context for Development.* London: Falmer Press.

Whitfield, R. (1994) *Report of the All Party Parliamentary Group on Parenting and International Year of the Family,* UK Parliamentary Hearings.

Chapter 10

Parenting education and support: issues in multi-agency collaboration

Peter Jones

Multiple agencies, multiple interests?

The meteoric rise of interest in parenting education and support in Britain during the 1990s has been premised on a diversity of approaches to meet a diversity of needs, rights, and responsibilities across many stakeholder interests. In this chapter I want to explore a framework for differentiating those interests and seeing how they may overlap or conflict in shaping service delivery. If we are to take seriously the word 'education' in this field then it is important to be able to relate those interests to the curriculum content of parenting programmes and to how participants determine desirable outcomes. Further, I want to consider which elements of process between 'parent educators' and the parents they work with might constitute an appropriate model of pedagogy for parenting education.

Parenting education and support holds relevance for all agencies with an interest in influencing some stage of our lives as children, parents, grandparents or members of differing forms of family and community networks. Based upon a life cycle model for parenting it appears to offer a convenient continuity linkage for those agencies to share expertise, combine agendas, avoid duplication of resources, and to develop coherent, collaborative services which complement and enhance the efforts of any single agency. The danger is that parenting education and support may be seen as a panacea which enables sometimes quite disparate public service agendas to sit comfortably together. If collaborative multi-agency practice in parenting education and support is to be a sustainable reality, then we need to be clear about what all participants, including parents, are bringing to it, what they hope to gain from it, and why education rather than therapy, coercion, or punishment is being chosen as a vehicle for support or for change.

Discourses for parenting education and support

The identity for the field has coalesced with some key texts (Pugh, De'Ath, Smith 1994, Smith 1996, Ferri and Smith 1996), with the creation of the national umbrella body of the Parenting Education and Support Forum in 1995, and with the important focus of attention upon parenting from the Labour Party before taking office (Straw and Anderson 1996) and subsequently as the government in power. That identity is complex and many faceted. Interpretations of, and understandings for, desirable practice and intended outcomes may conflict with each other, reflecting different agency discourses for parenting education and support. I am using 'discourses' here to mean language being used to shape, construct and convey social realities rather than used to describe or represent phenomena (Parker 1992, Curt 1994). Discourses are not always predetermined or clearly defined, but they grow to influence or constrain the way things are conceptualised. Discourses for parenting education and support carry implicit value judgements for the role of parents in society and for what is desirable in parenting practice. They will influence the content of parenting programmes and the selection of targeted outcomes.

So, for example, the current Home Office discourse for parenting education and support which emerges in the Parenting Order of the 1998 Crime and Disorder Act, with punitive sanctions against parents for their children's offending, differs from that say of a voluntary mutual support group for parents with children facing learning difficulties. Multi-agency collaborative practice in parenting education and support needs to clearly recognise that such conflicting agendas may have to come together constructively in the development of joint services. Can educational interactions demonstrate sensitivity to the demands of combining what may be a range of conflicting agendas?

I believe there is a need to identify and where necessary to isolate some of the contributing or competing discourses if the policy field is to be understood, if multi-agency collaboration is to be sustainable, and if evaluation of practice initiatives is to be feasible. For those within a particular agency discourse there may be assumptions about shared beliefs in other agencies as to what constitutes parenting education and support – or simply a reluctance to recognise alternative specific agendas for involvement.

Parent educators – an established tradition

Advice to parents on how to rear children is not a new phenomenon. Discourses for parenthood, childhood, and who or what might best inform the process of parenting have changed over time (Abbot 1993). Such discourses reflect the interests of many interacting systems in society and interpretations for balance between the rights of adults and children. They involve social constructions for childhood, for cultural allocation of who should be responsible for rearing children, and for the interrelations between the state and individual families in determining appropriate parenting behaviour. Predominant in the current discourses for parenting in Britain is that of parents as providers of a children's welfare service. Other cultures and historical times may place greater emphasis on that role being fulfilled by other family members, community members, or in greater or lesser part by the state. Pugh, De'Ath and Smith (1994) constructed a generic and comprehensive discourse for parenting education and support which achieved a distillation of views from a very wide sweep of heterogeneous research, policy and practice. Complexity is endemic to a field which via its life cycle model might be seen to apply across an individual parent's whole life span, and to relate to every government department and most areas of social policy at central and local levels.

Although there are common threads in many of the discourses for parenting education, choices for emphasis in promotion of parenting practice, or chosen targets for prevention, will reflect the agendas and interests of those controlling a particular discourse. Parenting and parenting education is an amalgam of sets of constantly evolving social constructions for parents, children, and social environments. Within the many interdependent discourses for parenting education and support there are implicit and explicit belief systems for what constitutes desirable developmental patterns for children's growth, learning, and social behaviour, for desirable parenting behaviour toward children, and for desirable parental states of health, social responsibility, moral responsibility, attitudes towards learning, spiritual and ethical beliefs, and so on. Making sense of the roles of parent *educators* needs to be sensitive to that complexity. Discourses with a prime focus on child-centred outcomes may construct parents and parenting very differently from discourses for empowerment of adults as parents needing adequate structural support, or for 'treatment' of adults not coping with stresses arising from parenthood, or which see parents as adult learners with constrained opportunities for learning. Those involved as parent educators need to be aware of competing discourses for adult rights, children's rights, and the rights of professional and paraprofessional groups to claim substantive knowledge within the field.

Espoused 'expert' knowledge for good practice in parenting reflects cultural milieux and historical determination of knowledge:

> Until the middle of the eighteenth century in Britain advice given to parents within the medical discourse for children's development favoured swaddling. Babies were tightly bandaged to keep them warm and help them to grow straight – it was not realised that

rickets, which affected many children, was caused by calcium deficiency. (Abbot 1993, p.27)

Similarly, parents were advised earlier this century 'to feed their babies on a rigid, pre-determined cycle of time intervals' (Truby King 1937); to give children sugar-laden NHS orange juice; and until very recently to lay their babies face down in their cots. That all such advice is now seen to have been at best misguided suggests, I think, not that the current state of received wisdom on parenting practice within the medical discourse is now necessarily better or more accurate, but that parents might reasonably assert caution in accepting prescriptive advice.

The whole of this century has seen the growth of psychology and its relationship to parents and children. It has strongly influenced social attitudes towards and understanding for all parent–child relationships. Its pervasive effect has been challenged in the emergence of counter strands against the reification of the 'psy' professions' shaping of knowledge for parenting, and dominance of knowledge for parenting education and support. The profession has been accused of creating 'expert' knowledge to meet their own disciplinary interests as much as the best interests of parents and children (Ingleby 1985).

I think it is important that we continue to raise questions as to which orthodoxy in parenting practice and patterns of child development is being promoted, and whether it precludes or denigrates any deviation from that practised by the *educator*, or that embedded in a particular discourse for parenting. It is important that the power for determining desirable styles of parenting does not reside solely with the state, with professional bodies, with community control mechanisms, with individual parents, or with the demand characteristics of individual children. Yet in recognising the contributions of each of these stakeholding positions there has to be recognition for the implicit value base and lability of understanding and knowledge which underpins each.

In pursuit of prevention

Discourses for parenting education and support may be premised upon, or make frequent reference to, interventions at several levels to prevent or reduce the effects of problems in such areas as health, learning and development, social, moral, or faith behaviours – for children or for parents themselves. The discourses vary in the way they balance *empowerment* for parents, *promotion* of particular aspects or outcomes of parenting, and *prevention* targets for others, though for statutory agencies the former two are more likely to be seen as means to achieve the latter than ends in themselves. Models of empowerment, promotion or prevention may need to differentiate between the needs of parents and the needs of children as beneficiaries [or victims] of parenting

Public health type models of prevention, based upon universal vulnerability to physical disease and intervention strategies such as immunisation or improved sanitation, are generally seen as desirable and non-stigmatising both to those funding intervention and to those benefiting by it. They do not transfer easily to a policy field such as parenting education and support. Even were sufficient funding available, convincing prospective parents of the value of focused preparation for parenthood or convincing existing parents of the need to reconsider their approach to parenting, to prevent problems arising for themselves or their children, calls for a significant shift in cultural acceptance of such support. This is particularly so when parents targeted are often in community locations already stigmatised by poverty, poor housing, prevalence of unemployment, high level of crime, domestic violence, and child abuse, etc., and in which those factors can be interpreted to powerfully influence the parenting process. Models of accident prevention or crime prevention, in which matrices of interacting risk factors in specific contexts are identified, targeted, and reduced, may increasingly determine a role that parenting education and support might best take in such contexts – the inclusion of parenting education as a component in the CTC (Communities That Care) programmes exemplifies such thinking (CTC (UK) 1997).

A conceptual map for the field

Given the diversity of interests informing the development of parenting education and support, and the diversity of intended outcomes, it may be helpful to attempt some overall framework which helps to map the interdependent conceptualisations of the field. Figure 10.1 is a first step in that process. Here I have conceptualised parenting education and support on the vertical dimension to be seen primarily as a service concerned with children's welfare or adult's welfare or some variable position between the two which accepts their essential inseparability.

As a child welfare service, parents are conceptualised as the prime agency in enabling the child's health, safety, learning and development, moral and spiritual welfare to be realised. 'Parents' here may include step-parents, temporary partners, grandparents, older siblings, and other carers fulfilling the parenting role for all or some of the time. They are the prime but not sole agency, and in extreme situations that agency may be removed by the state if protection of the child from abusive parenting is judged necessary. Parents are the prime agency, but are supported by other agencies

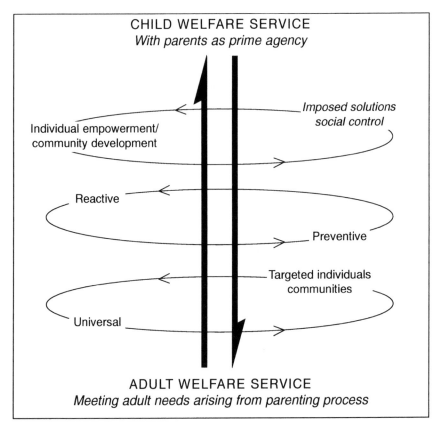

CHILD WELFARE SERVICE
With parents as prime agency

Imposed solutions social control

Individual empowerment/ community development

Reactive

Preventive

Targeted individuals communities

Universal

ADULT WELFARE SERVICE
Meeting adult needs arising from parenting process

Figure 10.1 A conceptual framework for parenting education and support

to promote the child's best interests. Within this model, multi-agency planning for parenting education and support might find best location in the development of Children's Services Plans, founded on the principle of parents as a partner agency not simply as service users. Discourses for emphasising this pole of the dimension may focus representation of the parenting selves of adults as:

- *stewards* for childhood or guardians of children's rights;
- *supervisors* of children's social behaviour and responsible for anti-social or criminal behaviour;
- *welfare* service providers, with particular focus on nurturing children during their early years, and to provide security, affection, material and psychological support for all areas of development;
- *educators* to help children make sense of learning experiences and develop independent thinking;
- *celebrants* of childhood or young adulthood, and facilitators of its freedoms;
- *models* for appropriate health behaviours, attitudes to learning, social and moral behaviours;

- *environmental controllers* for physical and social environments to prevent children's exposure to harm or harmful influence, and to allow contact with developmentally appropriate stimuli;
- *co-learners* with children.

This is not meant to be a comprehensive list, nor does it attempt to include the myriad roles that parents might adopt with and for children, and which different cultures or family groups may see to constitute desirable qualities in parents or parenting. It is rather a sample of what I see to be some key discourses which structure the way that parenting education and support is being conceptualised, each of which might be a dominant theme in a particular agency's agenda for involvement in the development of its policy or practice, or underpin any specific parenting programme or project. The discourses are interdependent, but may receive differing emphasis, or be seen to compete in multi-agency collaborations. Each might be reworded to imply strength or deficit modelling of parental selves to accord with service delivery interests for promotional, preventative, or reactive work.

At the other end of the vertical dimension, parenting education and support is seen as an adult welfare service to meet adult needs arising from the parenting process. These might include for example an emphasis on addressing post-natal depression, on maintenance of adult identity through social contact or adult learning paths, on information and advice for income supplements, employment rights, or change in housing, on guidance for adult relationships under stress from new parenthood, reconstitution of families, and so on. Discourses for the adult welfare pole of the dimension may focus representation of the parenting selves of adults as:

- *lacking preparation* for parenthood and psychologically stressed by its demands;
- *vulnerable parents* with learning or physical disabilities, physical or psychological illnesses;
- *social isolates* because of young age, minority ethnic status, or lone parent status;
- *denied freedom by lack of childcare* and unable to meet demands of paid employment because of lack of state provision of childcare or voluntary arrangements, or simply in need of a break from childcare responsibilities;
- *lacking self-esteem for learning and lack of self-fulfilment* which reflects a lack of achievement in their own learning and reduces their ability to promote their children's learning;
- *participants for mutual support networks* and/or development of shared childcare arrangements or children's facilities;
- *motivated towards community development* and able to see the need for community change to enhance environments for parenting and to challenge structural constraints to their children's development;

- *in need of empowerment* or consciousness-raising to avoid internalising blame for structural constraints to their parenting;
- *victims of their own parenting*, i.e. that which they received as children;
- *defined by gender stereotyping* of maternal or paternal roles and functions.

Again this is not meant to be an exhaustive list, and my comments on the child welfare pole list equally apply here. These are two poles of a continuum, and discourses relating to each are interdependent. However, in developing multi-agency collaboration I think it is important to raise awareness of these kinds of differences in understanding for what parenting education and support might seek to address in a particular practice, if development of that practice, or evaluation of its outcomes, is to gain coherence for a diversity of participants.

I have included three orthogonal axes to demonstrate the key conceptual dimensions informing models of service delivery in parenting education and support. They are drawn as ellipses with implied rotation to illustrate that (a) there is no assumed association between named poles across horizontal dimensions and (b) poles within dimensions are not always separable in practice and may co-exist whilst holding separate emphases. The dimensions are not arranged to imply hierarchical preference relative to the vertical axis, and should be seen as diagrammatically interchangeable. I have tried to avoid the compartmentalisation that a matrix format might convey.

This model is an attempt to map a 'feel' for this policy and practice space rather than to provide exact specification for forms that any programme of parenting education and support might take. Differing or competing agency agendas may place emphasis on different points of the given dimensions when seeking to influence parenting practice.

So, for example, the nascent Home Office *supervisors* discourse sees the role of parenting education and support to direct parents' attention to their prime agency role to look to their children's welfare by stopping their child re-offending. [Re-] education in parenting is a reactive response to children's criminal behaviour, targets individual parents, and is premised on imposing social control. The CTC (Communities That Care) alternative, whilst also seeing parents as *supervisors*, assumes their motivation towards *community development*. Similarly focusing on crime prevention, this conceptualises parenting education and support as one preventative strand amongst others in targeted communities of 10,000 to 12,000 people. It offers universal access within that community whilst invoking multi-agency support for community developmental approaches to meeting children's welfare needs.

In a primary school-based project to encourage parents to support their children's reading, a principal *educator's* discourse provides agency support to help parents meet children's welfare needs and prevent or reduce problems with literacy. Offering universal access for all parents of children in the school, some targeted individuals could be empowered to consider their own adult needs within a *lacking self-esteem for learning* discourse (e.g. Kemp and Neasmith 1992, Butt 1993).

A drugs information service specifically for parents might see several discourses overlapping. For children's welfare, discourses for parents as *models of appropriate behaviour* or as *environmental controllers* might depend upon an adult welfare discourse for parents *motivated towards community development* – it would depend enormously on which agencies were involved. The service would be likely to seek to empower parents, probably in targeted communities, to help prevent, reduce, or support constructive reactions to substance misuse (e.g. Marriott 1996).

Using a conceptual framework such as this serves to signpost the need for awareness of the diversity of forms that parenting education and support might take to reflect agency agendas and interests. With the increasing turn to ecological perspectives for understanding the multiple determinants for parenting (Luster and Okagi 1993), and with parenting in turn being seen as part of multiple determinacy for children's functioning, agendas for parenting education and support become multi-layered and changeable throughout the life cycle of parenting.

Identification and differentiation of discourses for parenting education and support is necessary if evaluation of multi-agency programmes of work is to progress beyond client satisfaction measures. Quality standards for practice in the field similarly need to recognise commonalities and differences in sets of process and outcome agendas from participating agencies. The model I have described here in part is an attempt to meet Weiss's (1995) call for bringing stakeholder assumptions to the surface if change process and outcomes in community level programmes are to be understood. It also, however, pursues VanderPlaat's (1995) thinking on the importance of surfacing conflicting positions, not attempting con- sensual agreement on an assumed ubiquitous outcome. Differing agency intentions, and differing constructions for parenting education, call for specification of clearly differentiated targeted outcomes, and measures specific to each agency agenda. Such specificity becomes increasingly essential if parenting education and support is to pursue a goal of statutory and voluntary agencies collaborating to provide coherent services for parenting, with preventative and reactive themes relating to each other.

Parent educators and pedagogy

Whatever the agency discourse for parenting education and support, and whatever the agency agendas it may be seen to fulfil, the implications of 'parenting education' for the identity of 'parent educators' need to be addressed. In various programmes of work the terms 'facilitator', 'group leader', 'support worker', 'catalyst', and so on, perhaps reflect some hesitancy in accepting those implications. This issue emerged at the launch of the Parenting Education and Support Forum in June 1995, when competing discourses surfaced in a debate as to what it should be named. The key conflicts were whether the word 'education' should be included and whether to choose 'parent' or 'parenting' as a lead word. The former was subject to constructions on continua from controlling/patronising to liberating/enabling, the latter to those for adult learning needs, or vocational preparation, through to adult–child process and challenge to contextual influences for the behaviour of both. The outcome was the mission statement definition of education as 'learning in the fullest sense, of growing in knowledge, skills, understanding and personal development' (PESF 1997). Yet though education without learning, or learners, would be a nonsense, it implies a whole set of other characteristic components, as important to parenting education as they are to other versions.

The sets of agency understandings for priorities in parenting, and intentions they carry in implementing parenting education, will shape the curriculum content and desirable outcomes for particular interventions. The process of education involves more than selection of content and target outcomes. It involves some individuals adopting the role of pedagogue as change agent. Learning is a social process, is does not occur in a vacuum, whatever the developmental stage of the learner, and it usually occurs with differentials in power or experience between teachers and learners. Pedagogy can be a formal or informal process, carried out by socially designated professional educators, or present in any interaction between two or more people in which learning is promoted by at least one to the others. It may be based in direct contact, implicit or explicit messages in social behaviour and environmental settings, or in media representation. Some stereotypical associations of pedagogy with dogmatism, control, and reification of book learning have perhaps confused the word with pedantry. Freire's (1970, 1996) use of the word to title his books on the importance of pedagogy to political liberation has hopefully shifted such perceptions.

Any single model of pedagogy for parenting education is unlikely to sit comfortably with all its constituent discourses. Agencies contributing to the funding of collaborative services in which parent learning is an intended outcome might reasonably seek reassurance that parent educators are able to use appropriate methods to meet a wide range of content and process requirements, and contextual demands. Schools-based approaches to preparation for parenthood might need to reflect established teacher–student interaction in host establishments, but parenting education with adults calls for pedagogic understanding which may differ significantly from adult basic learning, adult vocational learning, or adult higher education. I suggest starting points for a model of pedagogy for parenting education should include being able to:

- Provide opportunities for learning which wherever possible recognise parents and prospective parents' needs for choice of direction and duration of learning experience.
- Provide opportunities for parents and prospective parents to share experiences, to learn from, and to support each other.
- Value parents as prime agency for child's welfare but overtly state any agency agenda and beliefs of educator.
- Check for reciprocity in understanding of the intended outcomes of the learning situation.
- Offer information and skills teaching in interactional formats which allow for open discussion of differing value and belief systems.
- Promote meta-awareness of parenting process, to be able to look at how and why we might choose to parent the way we do.
- Demonstrate identification with 'good enough' states in parenting and not project personal experience of perfected skills and competencies.
- Sufficiently acknowledge macro-factors which may influence parenting in any given community, and facilitate access to relevant specialist advice when necessary, e.g. housing, welfare rights.
- Model desirable interactions for learning which parents could adopt with their children.
- Be organised around venues and times which recognise attention demands of childcare (e.g. take place within school hours, provide crèche facilities etc.).

Not all parents are confident about or motivated towards further learning about their parenting, even though an agency discourse might see such learning as desirable or essential. This may call for skills in adult education for a wide range of learners, and understandings for why and how learning in general takes place at many levels. Motivation for learning might be seen to reflect a level of developmental contentment – when a child or adult is content with the levels of knowledge and skills they possess, then motivation for change is diminished. For some parents motivation for learning in parenting education may be dependent upon available models of the 'next step' from other parents. It may call for sufficient interest in self-development, or belief that contextual constraints can be reduced, to create the wish to take that step, and some assurance that the step is not too big to take. Some parents may simply (and appropriately) wish for didactic transmission of information or advice, or for signposts to sources of further support. A key and difficult theme for parent educators working with individuals or groups may be to invite challenge to any 'expert' information or advice they are seeking to convey, or the way they are choosing to promote learning. Conversely, parent educators may be working with parents who are under some compulsion to attend and carrying externally imposed expectations that [re]learning will take place in a set period of time. It is important that agencies working together in parenting education and support, including parents, avoid assumptions that differing discourses for the field will not generate conflicts in what is deemed appropriate and acceptable practice in interactions to promote and facilitate learning about parenting. Effective models of pedagogy should frequently and overtly check for reciprocal understandings of purpose, content, and acceptable process between participants, and not be fearful of clarifying the agendas of those involved. Developments in the use of mediated learning experiences with adults and young people offer useful frameworks to inform such models (Feuerstein, Klein, Tannenbaum 1994).

Rhetorical support for coherent parenting education and support services in the late 1990s is not always matched by sustainable funding and resources. Existing individual statutory and voluntary agencies have their own histories, vested interests in owning areas of work, and specified responsibilities for child or adult welfare. Multi-agency collaborative practice in this field offers many opportunities for a new continuum of service delivery which could benefit all participants. This is more likely to become a practice reality if we pause to identify each of a possible cluster of understandings for what is being developed in a given context, identify commonalities and differences across stakeholder groups, and structure opportunities for learning which overtly recognise the range of participant agendas and responsibilities.

References

Abbot, M. (1993) *Family Ties: English Families 1540–1920.* London: Routledge.

Butt, A. (1993) *P.A.T.T.E.R. – Parents and Teachers Together as an Educational Resource.* ALBSU Newsletter, 49, Summer. London: Adult Literacy and Basic Skills Unit.

CTC (UK) (1997) *Communities That Care (UK): A new kind of prevention programme.* London: CTC (UK).

Curt, B. C. (1994) *Textuality and Tectonics: Troubling social and psychological science*. Buckingham: Open University Press.

Ferri, E. and Smith, K. (1996) *Parenting in the 1990s*. London: Family Policy Studies Centre.

Feuerstein, R., Klein, P. S., Tannenbaum, A. J. (eds) (1994) *Mediated Learning Experience (MLE): Theoretical, psychosocial and learning implications*, Second printing. London: Freund Publishing House.

Freire, P. (1970) *Pedagogy of the Oppressed*. New York: Continuum.

Freire, P. (1996) *Pedagogy of Hope: Reliving pedagogy of the oppressed*. New York: Continuum.

Ingleby, D. (1985) 'Professionals as socialisers: The "Psy-complex"', in Spitzer, S. and Scull, A. T. (eds) *Research in Law, Deviance and Social Control: A Research Annual*, vol. 7, 79–109. New York: JAI Press Inc.

Kemp, C. and Neasmith, P. (1992) *C.A.P.E.R. – Children and Parents Enjoy Reading*. ALBSU Newsletter, 46, Summer. London: Adult Literacy and Basic Skills Unit.

Luster, T. and Okagi, L. (eds) (1993) *Parenting: An ecological perspective*. New Jersey: Lawrence Erlbaum Associates.

Marriott, R. A. (1996) *"Positive parents" – Community Development as an approach to drug use within communities*. Talking Point, 168. August/September. Newcastle-Upon-Tyne: Association of Community Workers.

Parker, I. (1992) *Discourse Dynamics: Critical analysis for social and individual psychology*. London: Routledge.

P.E.S.F. (1997) *The Parenting Education and Support Forum Constitution*. London: Parenting Education and Support Forum.

Pugh, G., De'Ath, E., Smith, C. (1994) *Confident Parents, Confident Children – Policy and practice in parent education and support*. London: National Children's Bureau.

Smith, C. (1996) *Developing Parenting Programmes*. London: National Children's Bureau.

Straw, J. and Anderson, J. (1996) *Parenting: A discussion paper*. London: Labour Party.

Truby King, F. (1937) *Feeding and Care of Baby*, revised edition. London: Oxford University Press.

VanderPlaat, M. (1995) 'Beyond Technique: Issues in Evaluating for Empowerment', *Evaluation* **1**(1), 81–96.

Weiss, C. H. (1995) 'Nothing as practical as good theory: exploring theory-based evaluation for comprehensive community initiatives for children and families', in Connell, J. P., Kubisch, A. C., Schorr, L. B., Weiss, C. H. (eds) *New Approaches to Evaluating Community Approaches: Concepts, methods, and contexts*. Roundtable on Comprehensive Community Initiatives for Children and Families. New York: The Aspen Institute.

Chapter 11

'She wants you to think for yourself, she doesn't want to give you the answers all the time': parents on parenting education and support

Roger Grimshaw

Introduction

Increasingly, parenting education and support (PES) has been promoted as a service designed to meet the needs of a wide spectrum of parents. That assumption underpins the development of 'open access ' parenting programmes intended for any parent who wants to do an acceptable job of bringing up a child. Programmes have more than an educational function; they are also meant to provide the support that parents need. It is understandable if people hearing those claims are inclined to reach for the proverbial pinch of salt. Needs are notoriously difficult to define for all sorts of reasons: one person's necessity is another's luxury; different cultures or social groupings may highlight different needs; or fathers may have different needs from mothers. As commentators have been quick to point out, making PES widely available challenges the conventional wisdom that parenting is a natural function normally requiring no education (Cunningham 1996, Roe 1997, Hardyment 1997). By this definition, only parents with problems – or 'bad parents' – need such provision (Parkin 1997). So why offer it to anybody else? Advocates of a wider role for PES will counter that only the most exceptionally gifted parent will need no information or support at all.

These differences of view remind us that needs are socially constructed and can be controversial. In this chapter I want to shed some light on perceptions of need by drawing on the views of contemporary parents. I try to show how parents themselves give accounts of their needs which build on their conceptions and lived experiences. In a diverse society open access services should be capable of meeting a whole range of needs. Yet there is very little evidence about how ordinary parents define parenting, its problems and tensions, and seek to access help.

This chapter is intended to do two things: to give some insight into how contemporary parents view parenting needs; and to show how these perspectives inform their assessments of the parenting education and support that would be useful to them. It is based on a recent study of stakeholders' views, conducted by the National Children's Bureau and supported by the Joseph Rowntree Foundation (Grimshaw and McGuire 1998). The study sought to compare the views of different stakeholders in parenting programmes – funders, service commissioners, and managers; professionals who made referrals; programme facilitators; parents in touch with programmes and those who knew very little about them; and – not least – children. In this chapter I wish to devote space to parents' views, in order to illuminate their thinking and to question possible misconceptions about their needs.

The material of the chapter is derived from individual qualitative interviews with a sample of 55 parents, systematically selected to represent a range of identities and experiences. As a small-scale exploration of the field the research cannot support quantitative generalisations about the population as a whole. However it does identify certain structures of meaning and experience which could be used as analytical templates in larger studies. The methodology resembles the grounded theory building of Glaser and Strauss (1967), in that comparisons are made across groups and settings as a way of refining interpretations and moving toward conclusions.

I have already indicated that debates about parenting needs can polarise into two opposed fundamentalisms: antagonists of PES resent what they see as interference with a so-called natural function; protagonists prefer to emphasise how much all parents need to learn and to obtain support. Instead the study findings point to a rather more complex picture. They indicate the ways in which parents conceive parenting as an active process – a conscious path not simply a natural function. Indeed a range of parents see the potential in PES for further learning and mutual aid. But neither are they empty receptacles ready to be filled with the 'good things' offered by parenting services. PES initiatives need to be sensitive to the many possibilities of nurturing a growth and learning curve in which parents acquire greater control over their parenting, so giving them more informed choices.

The chapter begins with a profile of the parents in the interview sample. It examines in turn: their conceptions of parental responsibility; the extent to which they had learned to be parents; their experiences of stress; and the sources of help, support and information which they had used. Their views about parenting programmes are described, especially the outcomes they would like to experience. Finally the chapter considers the concept of the connected or empowered parent as a way of understanding more clearly how PES could be helpful.

Who were the parents in the study?

Interviews took place with a range of stakeholders associated with three parenting programmes selected from a national sample of programmes. The programmes were meant to represent a variety of geographical areas and potential users. Two were organised in health service settings and the third in a primary school.

To obtain a balanced picture, it was essential to interview not only parents who had attended programmes but also parents who had not. To elicit a range of relevant views, four categories of parent were interviewed: parents who had been on a course and attended most of the sessions (a total of 21 attenders); those who had only attended a small number of sessions (6 drop-outs); those who knew of a course but had decided not to participate (17 refusers); and a further 11 parents who were in effect excluded because they had not been made aware of the programme.

Of the 55 parents in the sample, 71 per cent were women, 78 per cent were white and the rest came from minority ethnic groups. The most highly represented minority group was African – six in all, including three war refugees. There were individuals from African-Caribbean, Indian, Bangladeshi and mixed backgrounds.

The majority had a partner, but nine per cent were parenting alone. Just over half (51 per cent) were couples (but were interviewed individually).

Just over half (54 per cent) had been parents for up to four years. Two-fifths (42 per cent) had been parents for five to ten years, while the remaining four per cent had been parenting for up to 15 years.

All household incomes were represented in the sample.

Weekly household incomes ranged from less than £100 to over £1,000.

The largest group (18 per cent) had an income between £300 and £400 per week.

Almost 50 per cent of the sample had an income below £400 per week.

Almost a fifth (18 per cent) fell into the lowest income category – up to £200 per week.

Further methodological details are given in the main report (Grimshaw and McGuire 1998).

Parents on parenting

'Be there for them'

This section suggests how parenting responsibility is defined in ways that transcend any particular function or purpose. Instead it is a general construct defining an enduring relationship with children.

What does parenting involve? In response to this broad question nearly all parents revealed a sense of responsibility or an attitude of care towards children. Mothers and fathers were saying much the same things.

'Responsibility is the first thing that comes to mind and I didn't realise what a responsibility it is and how much you affect your children.' (*Mother*)

'All your time, all your energy and all your efforts, a lot of hard work. It involves a lot of responsibility.' (*Mother*)

'I think it's a total and utter commitment not to be taken on too lightly' (*Father*)

Whereas society expects parents to maintain and support children in material terms, only seven parents in the sample mentioned this aspect. Controlling children was mentioned by just eleven. It was as if the core of parenthood was defined in terms of watchfulness and responsiveness – a global commitment rather than a specific function. Aspirations for their children were modest. Only a minority mentioned any particular educational or career goals. Parents nearly all envisaged their children adjusting to society – having a sense of right and wrong, being happy and so on.

'Hopefully, they'll grow up to learn what's wrong, what's right, get their own families, get married, have their own families one day, just be there for them basically.'

There was no clear evidence of social values motivating parents to seek help, so that, for example, their children would end up with particular advantages. The impression was of parents who took their responsibilities seriously, without analysing exactly what these might entail. Parenthood was therefore an open-ended commitment, which seemed to embrace the care of children without directing them towards a foreseeable future.

Stress

Fulfilling responsibilities often comes at a cost. At various points parenting is likely to become a stressful experience for the most well-resourced and adaptable parent. The interviews provided evidence of stresses, some predictable, others less so. Partly as an exercise to compare the various segments of the sample, a list of stressful situations was constructed by the research team, ranging from the parent's emotional, health, financial or housing problems to the strains of caring for a large or demanding family. A cumulative stress score was calculated for each parent based on evidence from the interviews.

- Fifteen parents, or just over a quarter of the sample, were judged to have had no such stresses at all.
- While three were rated as having a score between none and one, 14 had been subject to one stress.
- While two were rated as having a score between one and two, ten had been subject to two stresses.
- Eleven parents had been subject to more than two stresses and the most stressed individual disclosed seven.

Feelings of stress were not confined to one section of the sample, as one man described.

'And the only way I found for me, I am actually sad to admit it, was to put headphones on with the music on, loud enough so I couldn't hear him screaming. Lots of neat whisky for me [not him!] and I would sit there and cuddle him in my arms, rocking him, talking nicely and calmly, because as I say, it's just this screaming that triggers something in me.'

Analysis of the scores showed no significant differences between white and minority ethnic groups, men and women, or between attenders and non-attenders. Nonetheless it was clear that interviewees had experienced a whole range of stresses in different combinations while some appeared 'stress free'. From this point of view the group spoke from a wide spectrum of experience.

Learning to be a parent

When asked to describe the most difficult parts of being a parent, nearly all mentioned the demands of looking after a child.

'The energy to keep up with them! Patience, I think patience is the number one key, being really patient with them and try and make allowances for the fact that they are learning every single day.'

Asked to describe what they had had to learn about parenting, about two-fifths mentioned patience, a similar proportion referred to knowledge, but no less than a half referred to skills of caring.

These skills were essentially practical, for example, managing the child's attention in everyday circumstances.

'He likes..., drawing, he likes writing and he asks me how to spell things. I mean he can't spell, he can't write but he is like trying to keep things and you are doing one thing and he is asking you another, "Are you listening to me?" "Yes", as you are doing something else... It's trying to keep them occupied.'

A variety of ways of finding information were described – talking with friends, family and services. On balance there was a satisfactory outcome: only a tenth of the respondents felt they had little success in finding the information they required. But it was not a straightforward process. Services did not communicate clear expectations about early development and care needs. Resolving uncertainty of this kind meant that the parent herself had to search for information.

> 'They teach you how to bathe it , how to change its nappy, how to feed it and burp it and that's it. "Take it home, that's your baby." What do you do with it? Put it up on the kitchen table and look at it every day? [laughs]...They are learning how to do things and how to sit up but they don't teach you about things like that – what to expect...People automatically think that, "Oh because you are a mother, the information just comes to you just like that." It doesn't.'

> 'I think there is lots of responsibility and everybody expects you just to be able to perform. You know, you have these children; but nobody tells you what to do with them, although [it's] easy to have them, what to do with them when you've got them.'

> 'I have to learn everything really because I didn't have a clue. I have to learn from other people, just generally picking up on the ideas they've got.'

A mother of Asian origin summed up this process of learning as a conscious exertion.

Roger: Were there things that you had to learn about being a parent?
Mother: I don't think it is a natural process as some people seem to find it. I have not found it a natural process – that it just comes to you naturally. Something that I have to work at all the time and rethink really.

Part of this learning appeared to be about acknowledging the differences between children in the same family.

> 'whereas Simon is quite an introvert Elsa is extrovert. And they are so completely different. It is amazing to see that Simon is fussy about his food and he would not have butter on his bread and he only eats certain things; Elsa would eat anything.'

The parent's sense of responsibility was the spur to a process of learning which came by dint of effort rather than by natural enlightenment. This notion of individual responsibility seemed to generate an impulse to seek advice and help as well as a discriminating attitude to the help available.

Support, help and advice

Support to parents was primarily a function of their relationships with family and partners. Over two-fifths said that their biggest source of help was from family. The next largest – just less than a quarter – nominated their partner. The rest mentioned a combination of helpers. Few said they obtained most help from friends or a service.

The gender of parents seemed to be an influence on patterns of help. There was some evidence that men were more frequently inclined to nominate their partners than vice versa; women more frequently spoke about help from family. Likewise the majority of attenders mentioned help from family. This evidence tends to suggest traditional patterns of support: family members supported mothers, while fathers looked to their partners for help.

Parents were asked to describe the advice they had received from services such as GPs, health visitors, nurses or teachers and to comment on its helpfulness. A significant minority, typically men, had not received any such advice. Contacts with services were more frequently the responsibility of women. In fact only two of the men made any comments on services. Almost half of those who had contact with services rated the advice helpful, the others were less impressed and just an eighth were negative.

Besides services there are sources of advice in the mass media, particularly in parenting magazines and family-oriented TV programmes. Again a large proportion had not obtained advice from the media and those who had held a mixture of views, most showing qualified approval. Attenders were more likely than others to have found advice in the media but there was no difference in the proportion of men and women making comments, suggesting that both sexes are exposed to media messages. The availability of authoritative books on childrearing creates another source of advice. In fact a minority of the parents mentioned books they had used, like Penelope Leach's *Baby and Child* or Chris Green's *Toddler Taming* (Leach 1979, Green 1992), but most of the parents who commented were positive in their opinions of their value. On the whole it seemed that messages from the media and books were more likely to reach men directly than messages from services.

Despite the impulse to seek advice, what emerged quite strongly was the importance of personal judgement in handling the advice.

'Obviously [my parents'] views are totally different to mine and like [my husband] would sometimes tell me something that is totally different. So, at the end of the day, I have to go with my own feelings. I do try to listen to as many people as I can just to pick up ideas on what they are doing with their children.'

'Very rarely have I found people unwilling to give advice. In fact, you'll have more than enough people wanting to give you advice or "You shouldn't do this, or shouldn't do that. This is how you should do this.". . . But you've got to be able to sift out what makes sense to you and what seems right, what feels right to you.'

Parents filter the information made available to them, exercising judgements about what is appropriate to their children. It seems that precisely because of their sense of personal responsibility they are suspicious of generalisations that are not tailored to a knowledge of particular children and their particular characteristics.

Views on programmes

Given their ideas about parenting, how far did the parents in the study regard programmes as relevant to their needs? At what stage would access be useful? How should programmes be delivered? And what should they cover? What would be useful outcomes? The following section explores how far programmes can fit into the agendas of parents themselves, rather than an agenda imposed on them from outside.

The knowledge gap

Despite the attention given to parenting programmes in sections of the press, knowledge about them still seemed restricted. To clarify the public profile of programmes, parents interviewed were asked to identify any programmes for parents which they knew. Obviously, attenders, drop-outs and refusers knew about one course. A number of the sample mentioned parent-craft and antenatal classes. Apart from these, there was little awareness of parenting programmes. A few were aware of a course that a friend might have attended or knew of post-natal groups. But 35 parents (amounting to 70 per cent of those who replied) knew of nothing else at all, confirming the very low current profile of parenting programmes.

Parents had very little background information with which to assess the relevance of programmes in general or to evaluate what they were told by professionals associated with a particular programme.

Interest in programmes among non-attenders

The low visibility of programmes made it difficult to explore opinions about them in the way attitudes to well-known services can be investigated. So parents who had no contact with a programme were given some general information and invited to ask questions before their views were sought.

The level of interest which they expressed was relatively high (Table 11.1). A number would have wanted this service in the past but felt that it would not be appropriate now. Others would only want the service if they had a problem or they wanted more specific help. A few were more comfortable with a TV or video presentation.

Table 11.1 Interest in parenting programmes among non-attenders

Responses	N
Yes	12
Possibly in the past	5
Only if I had a problem	6
No	2
Can't attend	2
Other kind of service	1
TV/Video	2
Total	30

So what led parents to reject programmes? One explained that her unwillingness to use either services or groups was for two reasons: strong family support and her resistance to anxiety.

'I have never been one for mother and toddlers groups but I have such a large family. I have all that I need and sometimes I do think the mothers and toddlers groups are also for the mothers, you know the contact is there and the worries that they had or...I am not a worrier by nature.'

Her own mother she saw as a fount of wisdom.

'My mum is quite a ... wise woman and she puts [me] on the right track.'

Such self-confidence augmented by valued support and advice understandably diminished the appeal of programmes and so put the views of other parents in a contrasting light.

The best stage to attend

Parents who had attended sessions or expressed an interest in doing so were asked to say when they might prefer to take part.

Over half the respondents wished to access a programme before a child reached the age of three years.

'I found out about them by accident but I wish I'd found out about it earlier, a lot earlier, and I think perhaps, it's something they should hand out after you've had a baby or something, or at the health clinic, when you go up to weigh in and the health visitors should point these things out.'

The most popular option was to go on a programme in the child's first year – an idea with a particular appeal to women. Even among the parents with school age children there was a clear preference for an earlier opportunity to attend. Parents saw a programme as a timely foundation for their careers as parents, rather than something that could be equally beneficial at any time.

Leadership

Parents were asked to say what kind of person should be 'a leader'. Instead of simply opting for expertise, they expressed a strong preference for someone who was a parent, or who was both a professional and a parent.

Asked to describe the qualities of a leader, nearly all respondents mentioned qualities such as the ability to communicate and to listen, friendliness, patience, openness and compassion.

> '[My model leader] is an active listener actually, I think, which is what I like, if I am talking to someone. And the other thing, is, she wants you to think for yourself, she doesn't want to give you the answers all the time.'

The parents clearly wanted a friendly listening partner, as opposed to a didactic teacher.

Partners' participation

Most parents — both men and women — said they would wish their partners to accompany them. However, some were certainly doubtful, feeling that the group discussion would not be so frank or allow feelings to be expressed.

> 'I mean [my husband] went to Parent Craft with me but I wouldn't say he learned anything. I think it's somewhere where mums can let go and we can have a moan about the husbands.'

Fathers' programmes were not a popular choice. As one father put it:

> 'I just don't think it's in the male make-up to sit there and talk about, I suppose it's interesting for a little while but I don't think blokes tend to click so well.'

Help to attend

Accessing programmes remained a problem. When asked what help they might need, regardless of their preferences about attending with partners, a large majority mentioned childcare as a basic prerequisite for attendance. For single parents, cost might be a major deterrent.

> 'the only thing that I do suffer from is baby sitters, the young girl down the road costs me £5 each time I have a baby sitter. I am not in a financial situation to keep paying out £5 here and there for a baby sitter.'

Only an eighth of respondents mentioned their work arrangements and a similarly low proportion referred to a variety of needs. Hence childcare is a fundamental factor to be taken into account in considering programme access.

Content

The 51 parents with some interest or experience were asked what they wanted to be included in an ideal programme. Fourteen of those who had attended sessions opted for what they had experienced. Seven of the rest went along with what had been described to them. A mother of Asian origin suggested that the normal programme topics were relevant to most parents regardless of background.

'Most parents come acoss, whatever religion or background or whatever, they come across very similar problems, you know, teaching children good behaviour rather than bad behaviour, actively listening to children, what they are saying; these are things you come across whatever language you speak so your [...] sounds fine to me.'

Further options were explored with the respondents as the interview continued. About a quarter of the respondents expressed interest in family and social issues, in child behaviour and so on. A similar proportion wanted information about child development or health. Fewer – just one in ten – were interested in educational issues for their children. More personal topics and feelings were not raised. There were several other formulations or suggestions mentioned, such as targeting a particular age group of children. A single parent wanted a course specifically for single parents, suggesting the importance of considering individual needs in a group setting.

Views about outcomes

All parents interviewed, whether they had experience of programmes or not, were invited to say what they expected to get out of a programme (Table 11.2). The most frequently mentioned were group outcomes, such as comparing individual experiences with other people's.

Table 11.2 Outcomes envisaged by parents

Group outcomes		
Networks	Compare self with others	**43 references by**
Friends	Learn from other parents	**31 respondents**
Relationship outcomes		
Understanding child	Resolve problem	**38 references by**
Communication	Less conflict	**27 respondents**
Relationship		
Knowledge outcomes		
Health outcomes	Education	**30 references by**
Development		**25 respondents**
Emotional outcomes		
Less anxiety	Happiness	**26 references by**
Raise confidence	Less stress	**20 respondents**

These were followed, in order of frequency, by a better relationship with the children, greater knowledge, and emotional benefits.

The value of sharing experiences was a frequent theme.

'I think if you feel that other parents experience the same problem then it's not just your problem, you are sharing something and it's not just your children that are behaving like that.'

Crucially, parents were seen as active mediators of the ideas being discussed. They were responsible for interpreting the relevance of the ideas and applying them within their own family settings.

'You can only go by models. You can't really define everything you've got to do to be a parent...Children are different; parents are different; people's circumstances differ. But if you can put them as working models then you get people thinking.'

'Every child is different, obviously,...you've got to sort of see what sort of a child, like I got two children that are completely different. My daughter is quiet, shy; [my son] touches everything, he talks, he shouts, he is a different sort of character, so I've got to deal with two different people.'

Asked to state the most important outcome, parents spread their choices across these categories or chose more than one. Relationship outcomes were rarely specified on their own as a primary outcome.

Parents were then asked to envisage important outcomes *for their children*. Rather than seeing the programmes as a foundation for achieving particular goals, parents envisaged more direct influences on the mutual relationship of parents and children. The most frequent replies, from about half the respondents, mentioned improvements in the parent–child relationship, such as behaviour changes and understanding. Almost three out of ten referred to a child's emotions, such as happiness or greater confidence. Only one in ten mentioned particular aspects of a child's needs, such as being healthy, making educational progress or meeting special needs. Again, just as in talking about parenting in general, they focused on a global relationship rather than particular functions.

If outcomes are to extend in to the future, how should the immediate impact be defined and related to future tasks and challenges? Parents were invited to distinguish 'short-term' from 'long term' benefits. The short term meant any benefit occurring immediately or in the months following a programme. The long-term was defined as a period extending beyond a year after the course.

Many of the responses concerning the short term were repetitions of previously stated outcomes or combinations of these; a small proportion were more focused on equipping the parent for the future. Equipping the parents for the future was much more recognisable among the attenders' responses.

The long term was conceived by some as an extension of the process of achieving outcomes, rather than as a qualitatively new phase. A minority saw the implications stretching up to a child's maturity. There were several responses identifying combinations of benefits or various individual wishes.

Attenders again were more likely to acknowledge the need to 'keep it up', not to lose ground. Like the others, however, it appeared that they sensed the future as an open extension of the present. Their sense of the future as relatively unspecific is understandable. Unlike professionals, parents have before them few well-defined benchmarks, like curricular targets.

This is not to say that once having accessed a programme parents envisaged that all would be plain sailing. Some suggested that they should be contacted at a later date as a form of auditing progress. In fact, virtually half the sample said that they would find a follow up course useful. And a few thought they possibly might take up that option.

Conclusions

Parenthood is evidently defined by several social discourses, including medicine, law and the administration of welfare. From these perspectives parenthood can appear as a biological relationship, a set of duties towards children, or a normative standard against which individuals are judged. But none of these exactly captures the personalised emotional engagement of parenting relationships. The idea of natural parenthood appeals to this social perception implying that parents have an intuitive capacity to do the right thing founded on an intimate, conscientious knowledge of their children. It would be understandable if parents simply spoke in these terms. Clearly they do have a unique perspective on their children. Yet this closeness can be marred by a sense of isolation. This is the unsettling reverse side of individual parental responsibility. As children develop, parents may feel unsure of their bearings if they are unable to compare their experiences and so interpret their children's unfolding lives more clearly. Indeed the evidence of the study uncovers layers of uncertainty that parents address by seeking information, advice, help and support. Nor are such needs confined to particular groups. Like the present study, a recent survey of parents in a multi-ethnic London borough revealed significant needs for information about health, childcare and development (Nicholas and Marden 1997).

Instead of a polarity between the 'natural' and 'artificial' parent it may be helpful to propose a more enlightening distinction.

The isolated or disempowered parent
An isolated parent is the product of a society with a high value put on responsibility and self direction but little value on widely sharing knowledge and experience.

The connected or empowered parent
A connected parent can take decisions in the light of accessible information and support over which the parent has some choice and control.

The point of this distinction is not to exaggerate the problem or talk up the solutions: it is not as if every parent, deep down, feels lonely, nor does the connected parent represent some superior ideal. It is to suggest that parents while retaining their individuality are open to forms of social connection and that PES could become an acceptable vehicle for this empowerment.

Increasingly it is argued that the economic capital of a society is not sufficient to confer benefits on individual families; people flourish in societies that have high levels of social capital – networks of mutual support and trust that reduce isolation and encourage participation (Gillies 1997). Moreover parents with low income and education tend to have lower social capital (Moore 1998). The connected parent benefits from access to social capital and can play a part in fostering access for others.

Some may be persuaded that after epochs of 'natural' parenting we have fallen from grace. Anxiety about the family is reflected in concerns about possible parenting deficits associated with child abuse and emotional problems. Structural changes in the family and the organisation of work spark furious debates about the direction of social change and its effects on parents. Extensive publicity for bad news about the family stokes what some see as an atmosphere of millennial crisis (Cox 1996). However, it is equally possible to regard the anxiety as a symptom not of failure but of an enhanced concern for children which draws on deep emotional feelings about the preciousness of childhood in an otherwise disenchanted world (Beck 1992). From this perspective the news may not be all bad.

It would be a mistake to hark back to a fantasy golden age of harmony in which parents instinctively did the right thing. It is time to move beyond the doom-laden effusions of publicity and to understand more closely the contemporary life world of parents. Parenting presents itself as a natural world and therefore an unconsidered one. Yet in actuality parenting issues are the subject of conscious reflection, advice and support. Websites for parents may sound artificial – especially with titles like 'the cybermom' – but electronic noticeboards where parents post accounts of their problems and seek advice from their counterparts appear to express very down-to-earth contemporary needs (Williams 1999). Therefore it is not a giant step for parents to contemplate joining a supportive group in which ideas are shared and discussed. The key point is that groups should be open to ownership by parents themselves and be inclusive of their different identities.

However, the social forces isolating parents make connecting up very difficult, and create obstacles to the exercise of choice. Parents have to make do with the connections they can create for themselves. Day-to-day responsibilities certainly reduce their capacity to socialise in groups. Ironically it may be just those individuals who have the least support who may be prevented from accessing help because they have no one to look after their children while they attend a group. Conversely those who least need support may be best able to attend. Solving this puzzle will require a real effort of coordination on an unprecedented scale, though there are promising examples of community approaches which combine supportive and educational services in one centre (Pugh *et al.* 1994). Supporting parents in the future will mean nurturing dense and robust networks fostered by active partnership among social agencies, employers and the government. If current initiatives like Sure Start are to succeed they must release a set of collective energies that go beyond the input of professionals (Home Office 1998). Connecting up parenthood is not simply about organising a team of expert facilitators with programme ideas and leaflets. It will demand serious commitments from the state, the private sector and voluntary sources so that parents themselves are allowed the time and the capacity to communicate with and, above all, support one another.

References

Beck, U. (1992) *Risk Society: Towards a new modernity*, translated by Mark Ritter. London: Sage.

Cunningham, J. (1996) 'Mother's little helper', *Guardian* Section 2, 23 October.

Cox, R. (1996) *Shaping Childhood. Themes of uncertainty in the history of adult-child relationships*. London: Routledge.

Gillies, P. (1997) 'Social capital: recognising the value of society', *Healthlines*, September, 15–17.

Glaser, B. and Strauss, A. (1967) *The Discovery of Grounded Theory*. Chicago: Aldine.

Green, C. (1992) *Toddler Taming*. London: Vermilion.

Grimshaw, R. and McGuire, C. (1998) *Evaluating Parenting Programmes. A study of stakeholders' views*. London: National Children's Bureau.

Hardyment, C. (1997) 'Parenting classes teach us nothing', *Daily Telegraph Weekend*, 1 February, 13.

Home Office Ministerial Group on the Family (1998) *Supporting Families. A consultation document*. London: Stationery Office.

Leach, P (1979) *Baby and Child*. London: Penguin.

Moore, H. (1998) 'Families and health in the UK', in Royal Society of Arts/Health Education Authority *The Health Debate: commitment, participation and communication. Report of seminars October 1997 and February 1998.* London: RSA.

Nicholas, D. and Marden, M. (1997) *The Information Needs of Parents. Case study: parents of children under the age of five.* British Library Research and Innovation Report 56. London: The British Library.

Parkin, J. (1997) 'Help for the mother of all tantrums', *Times Weekend,* 5 April, 13.

Pugh, G., De'Ath, E., Smith, C. (1994) *Confident Parents, Confident Children. Policy and practice in parent education and support.* London: National Children's Bureau.

Roe, N. (1997) 'Now Sophie's not a naughty girl any more', *The Independent Tabloid.* 12 February, 8–9.

Williams, C. (1999) 'Question: Who killed off Dr Spock? Answer: The Net', *Guardian G2,* 13 January, 8–9.

Index

adolescence 20
agencies *see* multi-agency collaboration
"Agenda for Action" 4, 5, 10
Alexander, Titus
  Empowering Parents 119–20
All Party Parliamentary Group on Parenting
  42–3, 135
Andersson, A.E. and Sylwans, P. 76
Atkinson, A.E. and Elliott, L. 75
attachment 8, 21, 22, 25
  changing insecure patterns 96–7
  characteristics of 19–20, 94–5
  emotional competence 7
  from child to parent 94–6
  linking experience to development 90–91
  and parenting 91–2
  and parenting education 18

Ball, M. 49, 51–2
Barlow, J. 23–4
behavioural approaches 23–4
behavioural theories 18
Bowlby, John 7, 91, 94
Brannen, J. and Moss, P. 75

capitalism 76–7, 78, 80, 100
Carpenter, B. 52
child abuse 6, 10
childhood 80–82, 85–6
Childline 35
children
  as co-constructors 85
  construction of the child 83–4
  and crime see crime
  in developmental psychology 82–3
  effect of divorce on 39
  and Family Law Act (1996) 9
  and homelessness 42
  and media education 72
  and non-maternal care 84
  and poverty see poverty
  reasons for running away 42
  responsibility of mothers 83, 84
Children's Services Plans 6, 49, 142
cognitive theories 18
cohabitation, and marriage 35–6, 42
Coleman, John 132
communities
  and family support 8, 11, 19, 20
  and parental support 4
Communities That Care (CTC) 141, 144
control, social 10, 144
cost benefit analysis 25–7
Cowan, Carolyn 23, 40
Cowan, Philip 23, 40
crime 8
  juvenile offending 6, 9–10, 23, 26–7
  and parental supervision 42, 144
Crime and Disorder Act (1998) 9, 23, 42, 138

Dahlberg, G. 81, 86
Dale, N. 54–5
Dawn Project The 96
Department of Health 6, 7
developmental psychology 82–3
DfE (Department for Education) 7

The Learning Age 7
divorce 37–9, 40, 41, 43–4
Dwivedi, K. 55–6
Dyson, A. 51

early years, importance of 6–7
Early Years Development and Child Care
  partnerships 6
education, definition 146
Einzig, H. 13, 17, 20, 43
Elmira home visiting study 25
emotional literacy
  emotions at work 99–100
  from child to parent 94–6
  parental sensitivity 93–4
  and parenting programmes 91
  and prospective parents 97–8
  qualities associated with 90
  reconnected with rationality 101
  role of caregivers 92–3
  through education 98–9
  wider context 100–101
emotional stress 94
emotions 4, 7, 21–2
employment see parental employment
empowerment 4, 6, 10, 14
evaluation
  of parental support 20–21, 126–7, 129–30
  of parenting programmes 22–5, 27–8, 43,
  112–14

families
  access to advice 8
  breakdown in 6, 8, 21
  centrality of family life 33–4
  changing dynamics 34–6
  and communities 8, 11, 19, 20
  financial support for 8–9
  interests of children 38–9
  intervention in 6, 13
  lack of role clarity 40–41
  and parental employment 9, 14, 34–5
  and parenthood 35–6
  and personal fulfilment 36–8
  serious problems in 9, 14
  step-relationships 41
  structure of 20, 33–4
  see also divorce; marriage; supporting
  families
Family Circle magazine survey 63, 69
"family friendly" approaches 52
Family Law Act (1996) 9, 43
Family Links project 50
Family Nurturing Network 24, 26
Family Policy Studies Centre 125
fathers 4, 10, 16
  and divorce 40, 41
Fraiberg, Selma 96
Frith, Simon 71

Giddens, A. 36–7
Giroux, H. 80
government
  and family support 6, 7, 43, 138
  political pressure by 23
  shifts in policy 6, 10, 13

grandparenting 41, 124
Grimshaw, R. and McGuire, C. 21, 151
Gurevitch, M. and Blumler, J.G. 63

Harvey, D. 76, 79
Health, Department of 6, 7
Hearn, B. and Sinclair, R. 49
Henggeler, Scott 26–7
HighScope 7, 25
Hinton, Sonya 125
    ABC of Behaviour 125, 126
    ABC Workshops 125
    Living with Teenagers 125, 132
Hinton, Sonya and Taylor, A.
    Getting Ready for School 125, 129
    Making the Move 125, 131
    Right from the Start 125, 128
Hochschild, A.
    The Time Bind 77
Home Office 138, 144, 164
    Family Support Grants 16
Home Start UK 20
Home-School Agreements (HSA) 49–50
homelessness 42
Hutton, W. 75

individualism 37
information needs of parents 44, 51, 162
Integrative Model of parenting education 24–5, 27
International Year of the Family (IYE) 5
intervention 6, 10, 20
    early 8, 12, 20
    empowerment model of 14
    group 14–15

Labour government see government
Long, Nicholas 22

McCarraher, L. 61
    Family Viewing 61, 73
Maines, B. and Robinson, G.
    Big School 131
Malaguzzi, Loris 85, 86, 88
marriage
    and cohabitation 35–6, 42
    modern 36–7
    and quality of parenting 40
    strengthening of 9
media
    broadcast 64–8
    children's education in 72
    current culture 62–4
    and parenting issues 67–70
    preferred information sources 71
    print 69–70, 156
    research 61–2
    role models in 70–71
    television's help to parents 64–6
    ways forward 71–3
mental health 6, 17
modelling 21
Moss, P. and Petrie, P. 83–4
mothers
    in employment 34–5
    responsibility for children 83, 84
motivation for learning 147–8
multi-agency collaboration 6, 15, 19, 27, 51–2
    competing discourses 138
    conceptual map 141–5

model of pedagogy 147
multiple interests 137
parent educators 138–40, 146–8
    for prevention 140–41
multi-cultural diversity 55–6
Multi-Systematic Therapy (MST) 26–7

National Childcare Strategy 9
National Children's Bureau
    performance indicators 55
    study of stakeholders' views 151
National Curriculum 7
National Family and Parenting Institute 5, 6, 8, 55
Negotiating Model 55
Newham
    extension project parenting programmes 109–11
        Caring Start 109, 110, 119
        evaluation 112–14
        Parent Link 109, 110
        seminar on lifelong learning 117–18
        Theatre Venture 114–17
    parenting education in 17–18, 50, 119–21, 107–9
        Learning Community Strategy 108, 117
        "Parents as Partners in Education" 108
        results of earlier successes 118–19
NEWPIN centres 21, 26

OFSTED inspection process 49

Parent Partnership Schemes 49
parent training, versus parenting education 22–5
parental employment
    major trends in 75
    mothers at work 34–5
    and parental support 87
    and parenthood 75–9
    and socio-economic change 76–7
    work-family relationship 9, 14, 34–5, 77–9
parental supervision, and crime 42, 144
parental support 20–22, 155–7
    aims 21
    areas of operation 4
    in children's education 7
    in community activities 4, 20
    of emancipatory nature 87
    emotions in parenting 21–2
    and employment 87
    evaluation of 20–21, 126–7, 129–30
    patchiness of 13, 16–17
    and resilience 19
    seen as normal 5
    by society 3
parenthood
    and employment 75–9
    and families 35–6
    nature of 162
    politics of 79–81
parenting education
    "Agenda for Action" 4, 5, 10
    and attachment 18
    behavioural theories 18
    defined 3–4, 13–14
    early studies 3
    group-based programmes 14–15
    integrative approach to 24–5, 27

local groups 16
in Newham see Newham
organisations for 16
in Oxfordshire 17
"permitting circumstances" 5, 19
principles for 4, 13–14
promotional model 27
and resilience 19
in Southern Derbyshire 17
uncoordinated local provision 16–17
value base of 4
versus parent training 22–5
workers 10
see also multi-agency collaboration; National
Family and Parenting Institute; Parenting
Education and Support Forum Parenting
Education and Support Forum 5–6, 16, 62,
138, 146
Parenting Forum 8, 16, 17, 55
parenting issues, and media 67–70
Parenting Orders 9, 23, 42, 138
Parenting Plans 44
parenting programmes
cost benefit analysis 25–7
emotional literacy 91
evaluation of 22–5, 27–8, 43, 112–14
factors influencing interest 90
incorporating diversity 55–6
key policy questions 43
parents views on 157–62
polarisation between 23–4
see also Newham; Surrey
parents
consultation about needs 48–51, 53–5,
150–51
differing roles 142–3
effect of divorce 39, 40–41
helped by television 64–6
information needs 44, 51, 162
isolated or connected 162–4
as learners 18, 154–5
on parenting 152–7
on parenting programmes 157–62
single see single parents
in stakeholders' study 151–2
as team partners 52
see also media; parental support
partnership model of services 52–5
PES (parenting education and support) 150–51,
163
PIPPIN 26, 96, 97–8
polarisation, between parenting programmes
23–4
politics
of childhood 80–82
government see government
of parenthood 79–84
Portage 50
poverty 5, 8–9, 10, 11, 25
prevention 11, 25, 27
multi-agency work 25, 27
primary 6, 20, 24
promotional model 27–8
Prout, A. and James, A. 82–3
psychology
developmental 82–3
growth of 140

Pugh, G., De'Ath, E. and Smith, C.
Confident Parents, Confident Children 3, 4,
13–14, 139 Quality Protects initiative 10

RAND Corporation study 26
Reggio-Emilia 85–6, 88
resilience 19, 25
Reynolds, J. and Mansfield, P. 37
Rodgers, B. and Pryor, J. 39
Rotherham projects 15

schools 4, 10
Sennett, Richard
Corrosion of Character 78, 100
services
and inclusivity 55–6
partnership model of 52–5
Shankill Road Early Years Project 15, 96,
100–101
Sinclair, R., Hearn, B. and Pugh, G. 7, 52
single parents 5, 20
Smith, C.
Developing Parenting Programmes 14, 16,
18, 21, 43, 124
social constructionist approach 86
social control 10, 144
social problems 9, 14, 34, 39
special needs education 50, 51
step-relationships 41
Stern, Daniel 92
stress 94, 133–5, 153
supporting families 6, 7–10, 42–4
and communities 8, 11, 19, 20
and government 6, 7, 43, 138
Supporting Families (Green Paper) 7–10, 33,
55, 78
supporting parents see parental support
Sure Start 7, 8, 11, 15, 27, 164
Surrey Educational Psychology Service 122,
125, 128, 132
Surrey LEA, parental support
at transitional times 122–3, 124–5, 135
family life cycles 123–4
what parents want 124
in early years 125, 129–30
evaluation study 126–7
managing behaviour 125–7
moving to secondary school 131
starting school 127–8
in teenage years 131–3
reducing examination stress 133–5
Svanberg, Per O.G. 20, 23, 25–6, 28

Talay-Ongan, A. 52
television
as help to parents 64–6
and parenting issues 67–8
theories, behavioural 18
Thomas Coram Foundation 21, 27
Trust for the Study of Adolescence 132
UN Convention on the Rights of the Child 10
VanderPlaat, M. 145
violence 6, 10

Waller, I. 26
websites 163
White, D. and Woollett, A. 122–3
Winnicott, Donald 92
Wolfendale, Sheila 50, 54, 113–14

UNIVERSITY OF WALES COLLEGE NEWPORT
LIBRARY AND INFORMATION SERVICES
CAERLEON